The unhappy favourite, or, The Earl of Essex a tragedy ... / written by John Banks. (1699)

John Banks

The unhappy favourite, or, The Earl of Essex a tragedy ... / written by John Banks.
Banks, John, d. 1706.
"Acted at the Theatre-Royal by Their Majesties servants."
"Epilogue" (p. [2] at end) by John Dryden.
Page 17 misnumbered 71.
[8], 62, [2] p.
London : Printed for Richard Wellington ... and Edmund Rumball ... and sold by Bernard Lintot ..., [1699]
Wing / B666
English
Reproduction of the original in the Bodleian Library

Early English Books Online (EEBO) Editions

Imagine holding history in your hands.

Now you can. Digitally preserved and previously accessible only through libraries as Early English Books Online, this rare material is now available in single print editions. Thousands of books written between 1475 and 1700 and ranging from religion to astronomy, medicine to music, can be delivered to your doorstep in individual volumes of high-quality historical reproductions.

We have been compiling these historic treasures for more than 70 years. Long before such a thing as "digital" even existed, ProQuest founder Eugene Power began the noble task of preserving the British Museum's collection on microfilm. He then sought out other rare and endangered titles, providing unparalleled access to these works and collaborating with the world's top academic institutions to make them widely available for the first time. This project furthers that original vision.

These texts have now made the full journey -- from their original printing-press versions available only in rare-book rooms to online library access to new single volumes made possible by the partnership between artifact preservation and modern printing technology. A portion of the proceeds from every book sold supports the libraries and institutions that made this collection possible, and that still work to preserve these invaluable treasures passed down through time.

This is history, traveling through time since the dawn of printing to your own personal library.

Initial Proquest EEBO Print Editions collections include:

Early Literature

This comprehensive collection begins with the famous Elizabethan Era that saw such literary giants as Chaucer, Shakespeare and Marlowe, as well as the introduction of the sonnet. Traveling through Jacobean and Restoration literature, the highlight of this series is the Pollard and Redgrave 1475-1640 selection of the rarest works from the English Renaissance.

Early Documents of World History

This collection combines early English perspectives on world history with documentation of Parliament records, royal decrees and military documents that reveal the delicate balance of Church and State in early English government. For social historians, almanacs and calendars offer insight into daily life of common citizens. This exhaustively complete series presents a thorough picture of history through the English Civil War.

Historical Almanacs

Historically, almanacs served a variety of purposes from the more practical, such as planting and harvesting crops and plotting nautical routes, to predicting the future through the movements of the stars. This collection provides a wide range of consecutive years of "almanacks" and calendars that depict a vast array of everyday life as it was several hundred years ago.

Early History of Astronomy & Space

Humankind has studied the skies for centuries, seeking to find our place in the universe. Some of the most important discoveries in the field of astronomy were made in these texts recorded by ancient stargazers, but almost as impactful were the perspectives of those who considered their discoveries to be heresy. Any independent astronomer will find this an invaluable collection of titles arguing the truth of the cosmic system.

Early History of Industry & Science

Acting as a kind of historical Wall Street, this collection of industry manuals and records explores the thriving industries of construction; textile, especially wool and linen; salt; livestock; and many more.

Early English Wit, Poetry & Satire

The power of literary device was never more in its prime than during this period of history, where a wide array of political and religious satire mocked the status quo and poetry called humankind to transcend the rigors of daily life through love, God or principle. This series comments on historical patterns of the human condition that are still visible today.

Early English Drama & Theatre

This collection needs no introduction, combining the works of some of the greatest canonical writers of all time, including many plays composed for royalty such as Queen Elizabeth I and King Edward VI. In addition, this series includes history and criticism of drama, as well as examinations of technique.

Early History of Travel & Geography

Offering a fascinating view into the perception of the world during the sixteenth and seventeenth centuries, this collection includes accounts of Columbus's discovery of the Americas and encompasses most of the Age of Discovery, during which Europeans and their descendants intensively explored and mapped the world. This series is a wealth of information from some the most groundbreaking explorers.

Early Fables & Fairy Tales

This series includes many translations, some illustrated, of some of the most well-known mythologies of today, including Aesop's Fables and English fairy tales, as well as many Greek, Latin and even Oriental parables and criticism and interpretation on the subject.

Early Documents of Language & Linguistics

The evolution of English and foreign languages is documented in these original texts studying and recording early philology from the study of a variety of languages including Greek, Latin and Chinese, as well as multilingual volumes, to current slang and obscure words. Translations from Latin, Hebrew and Aramaic, grammar treatises and even dictionaries and guides to translation make this collection rich in cultures from around the world.

Early History of the Law

With extensive collections of land tenure and business law "forms" in Great Britain, this is a comprehensive resource for all kinds of early English legal precedents from feudal to constitutional law, Jewish and Jesuit law, laws about public finance to food supply and forestry, and even "immoral conditions." An abundance of law dictionaries, philosophy and history and criticism completes this series.

Early History of Kings, Queens and Royalty

This collection includes debates on the divine right of kings, royal statutes and proclamations, and political ballads and songs as related to a number of English kings and queens, with notable concentrations on foreign rulers King Louis IX and King Louis XIV of France, and King Philip II of Spain. Writings on ancient rulers and royal tradition focus on Scottish and Roman kings, Cleopatra and the Biblical kings Nebuchadnezzar and Solomon.

Early History of Love, Marriage & Sex

Human relationships intrigued and baffled thinkers and writers well before the postmodern age of psychology and self-help. Now readers can access the insights and intricacies of Anglo-Saxon interactions in sex and love, marriage and politics, and the truth that lies somewhere in between action and thought.

Early History of Medicine, Health & Disease

This series includes fascinating studies on the human brain from as early as the 16th century, as well as early studies on the physiological effects of tobacco use. Anatomy texts, medical treatises and wound treatment are also discussed, revealing the exponential development of medical theory and practice over more than two hundred years.

Early History of Logic, Science and Math

The "hard sciences" developed exponentially during the 16th and 17th centuries, both relying upon centuries of tradition and adding to the foundation of modern application, as is evidenced by this extensive collection. This is a rich collection of practical mathematics as applied to business, carpentry and geography as well as explorations of mathematical instruments and arithmetic; logic and logicians such as Aristotle and Socrates; and a number of scientific disciplines from natural history to physics.

Early History of Military, War and Weaponry

Any professional or amateur student of war will thrill at the untold riches in this collection of war theory and practice in the early Western World. The Age of Discovery and Enlightenment was also a time of great political and religious unrest, revealed in accounts of conflicts such as the Wars of the Roses.

Early History of Food

This collection combines the commercial aspects of food handling, preservation and supply to the more specific aspects of canning and preserving, meat carving, brewing beer and even candy-making with fruits and flowers, with a large resource of cookery and recipe books. Not to be forgotten is a "the great eater of Kent," a study in food habits.

Early History of Religion

From the beginning of recorded history we have looked to the heavens for inspiration and guidance. In these early religious documents, sermons, and pamphlets, we see the spiritual impact on the lives of both royalty and the commoner. We also get insights into a clergy that was growing ever more powerful as a political force. This is one of the world's largest collections of religious works of this type, revealing much about our interpretation of the modern church and spirituality.

Early Social Customs

Social customs, human interaction and leisure are the driving force of any culture. These unique and quirky works give us a glimpse of interesting aspects of day-to-day life as it existed in an earlier time. With books on games, sports, traditions, festivals, and hobbies it is one of the most fascinating collections in the series.

The BiblioLife Network

This project was made possible in part by the BiblioLife Network (BLN), a project aimed at addressing some of the huge challenges facing book preservationists around the world. The BLN includes libraries, library networks, archives, subject matter experts, online communities and library service providers. We believe every book ever published should be available as a high-quality print reproduction; printed on-demand anywhere in the world. This insures the ongoing accessibility of the content and helps generate sustainable revenue for the libraries and organizations that work to preserve these important materials.

The following book is in the "public domain" and represents an authentic reproduction of the text as printed by the original publisher. While we have attempted to accurately maintain the integrity of the original work, there are sometimes problems with the original work or the micro-film from which the books were digitized. This can result in minor errors in reproduction. Possible imperfections include missing and blurred pages, poor pictures, markings and other reproduction issues beyond our control. Because this work is culturally important, we have made it available as part of our commitment to protecting, preserving, and promoting the world's literature.

GUIDE TO FOLD-OUTS MAPS and OVERSIZED IMAGES

The book you are reading was digitized from microfilm captured over the past thirty to forty years. Years after the creation of the original microfilm, the book was converted to digital files and made available in an online database.

In an online database, page images do not need to conform to the size restrictions found in a printed book. When converting these images back into a printed bound book, the page sizes are standardized in ways that maintain the detail of the original. For large images, such as fold-out maps, the original page image is split into two or more pages

Guidelines used to determine how to split the page image follows:

• Some images are split vertically; large images require vertical and horizontal splits.
• For horizontal splits, the content is split left to right.
• For vertical splits, the content is split from top to bottom.
• For both vertical and horizontal splits, the image is processed from top left to bottom right.

THE
Unhappy Favourite:
OR, THE
Earl of ESSEX.
A
TRAGEDY:
Acted at the
Theatre-Royal,
By Their Majesties Servants.

Written by *John Banks*.

——— *qui nimios optabat Honores,*
Et nimias poscebat Opes, numerosa parabat
Excelsæ turris tabulata, unde altior esset
Casus & impulsæ præceps immane Ruinæ. Juven. Sat. 10.

London: Printed for *Richard Wellington*, at the *Lute*, in St. *Paul's*
Church-yard; and *Edmund Rumball*, at the Post-House, in *Covent-Garden*; and
sold by *Bernard Lintot*, at the *Cross-Keys*, in St. *Martin's-Lane*, near *Longacre*.

THE
Unhappy Favourite:
OR, THE
Earl of ESSEX.
A
TRAGEDY:
Acted at the
Theatre-Royal,
By Their Majesties Servants.

Written by *John Banks*.

———— qui nimios optabat Honores,
Et nimias poscebat Opes, numerosa perabat
Excelsæ turris tabulata, unde altior esset
Casus & impulsæ præceps immane Ruinæ. Juven. Sat. 10.

London: Printed for *Richard Wellington*, at the *Lute*, in St. *Paul's*
Church-yard; and *Edmund Rumball*, at the Post-House, in *Covent-Garden*; and
sold by *Bernard Lintot*, at the *Cross-Keys*, in St. *Martin's-Lane*, near *Longacre*.

To the Moſt High, and Moſt Illuſtrious

PRINCESS,

The LADY

ANNE,

Daughter to His

Royal Highneſs.

MADAM,

I Humbly lay before your Highneſs Feet an Unhappy Favourite, but 'tis in Your Power to make him no longer ſo; Not his Queens Repentance, nor her Tears cou'd Reſcue him from the Malice of his Enemies, nor from the violence of a moſt unfortunate Death; but your Highneſs, with this unſpeakable Favour, and ſo Divine a Condeſcention in Protecting this once pity'd Hero, will make him live Eternally; and thoſe who cou'd ſcarce behold him on the Stage without weeping, when they ſhall ſee him thus exalted, will all

turn

turn envious of his Fortune, which they can never think deplorable while he is grac'd by your Highnefs. For my own part, I tremble to exprefs my Thanks in fo mean Language, but much more when I wou'd pay my Tribute of juft Praifes to your Highnefs; 'tis not to be attempted by any Pen, Heav'n has done it to a Miracle in your own Perfon, where are Written fo many admirable Characters, fuch Illuftrious Beauties on a Body fo Divinely fram'd, that there is none fo Dull and Ignorant, that cannot read 'em plainly. And when You vouchfafe to caft your Eyes on thofe beneath You, they fpeak their own Excellencies with greater Art and Eloquence, and attract more Admiration than ever *Virgil* did in his Divineft Flight of Fancy, than *Ovid* in fpeaking of his Princefs, or *Appelles* in drawing of his *Venus*: Nor are Your Vertues, or Your Royal Blood lefs admirable, fprung from the Ineftimable Fountain of fo many Illuftrious *Plantagenets*, that I ftand amaz'd at the Mightinefs of the Subject which I have chofen; befides the awful Genius of your Highnefs, bids me beware how I come too near, left I prophane fo many Incomparable Perfections in fo Sacred a Shrine

as

The Dedication.

as Your Highnefs Perfon, where You ought
to be ador'd, and not feen: For, like the Ancient Jews in their Religious Worfhip, 'tis a Favour for me to remain on the outward fteps, and
not approach nigh the Vail where the Croud never
come: This, moft Illuftrious Princefs, ought to
check my hand, left in attempting your Highnefs
Character, my Apprehenfion of the Excellence of
the Subject, and the danger of mifcarrying, fhould
make my Fancy fink beneath fo Glorious a Burthen; Therefore I will forbear troubling your
Highnefs any further with the Rafhnefs of my
Zeal; nor dare I be dictated any longer by it, but
will conclude, in hopes that, when hereafter I
may chance to Record the Memory of a Princefs,
whofe Beauty, Fortune and Merits are greater
than *Homer* ever feign'd, or *Taffo* Copy'd, I may
have leave to draw her Pattern from yourHighnefs,
and when that is done, the reft of my Life fhall
be imploy'd in Prayers for your Eternal Happinefs,
which be pleafed to interpret as the Duty of,

MADAM,

Your Highnefs's Moft Obedient,
Moft Humble, and
Moft Devoted Servant,

John Banks.

Persons Represented.

The Earl of Essex.	Mr. Clark.
Earl of Southampton.	Mr. Gryffin.
Burleigh.	Major Mohun.
Sir Walter Rawleigh.	Mr. Disney.
Lieutenant of the Tower.	

Queen Elizabeth.	Mrs. Quyn.
Countess of Rutland Secretly Married to the Earl of Essex.	Mrs. Cook.
Countess of Nottingham.	Mrs. Corbett.

Women.
Gentlemen, Guards and Attendants.

SCENE

WHITE-HALL,

AND THE

TOWER.

PROLOGUE,

Spoken by Major *Mohun*, the First Four Days.

THE Merchant, *joyful with the Hopes of Gain,*
   Ventures his Life and Fortunes on the Main ;
But the poor Poet oftner does Expose
More than his Life, his Credit, for Applause.
The Play's his Vessel, and his Venture, Wit :
Hopes are his Indies, Rocks and Seas, the Pit.
Yet our good-natur'd Author bids me swear
He'll Court you still, the more his Fate draws near ;
And cannot chuse but blame their Feeble Rage
That Crow at you, upon their Dunghill Stage ;
A certain sign they merit to be Curst,
When, to excuse their faults, they cry Whore first.
So oft in their dull Prologues, 'tis exprest,
That Critick now's become no more a Jest ;
Methinks Self-interest in 'em more should Rule ;
There's none so impudent to ask a Dole,
And then to call his Benefactor Fool ?
They Merit to be Damn'd as well as Poor,
For who that's in a Storm, and hears it roar,
But then would Pray, that never pray'd before ?
Yet Seas are calm sometimes ; and you like those,
Are necessary Friends, but Cursed Foes :
But if amongst you all he has no Friend,
He humbly begs that you would be so kind,
Lay Malice by, and use him as you find.

PRO-

PROLOGUE

Spoken to the K I N G and Q U E E N at their Coming
to the Houfe, and written on purpofe

By Mr. *D R Y D E N.*

WHEN firft the Ark was Landed on the Shore,
    And Heav'n had vow'd to curfe the Ground no more;
When Tops of Hills the Longing Patriarch faw,
And the new Scene of Earth began to draw;
The Dove was fent to View the Waves Decreafe,
And firft brought back to Man the Pledge of Peace:
'Tis needlefs to apply when thofe appear
Who bring the Olive, and who Plant it here.
We have before our Eyes the Royal Dove,
Still Innocence is Harbinger to Love,
The Ark is open'd to difmifs the Train,
And People with a better Race the Plain.
Tell me you Powers, why fhould vain Man purfue,
With endlefs Toil, each Obj&ct that is new,
And for the feeming fubftance leave the true ———
Why fhould he quit for hopes his certain good,
And loath the Manna of his daily food?
Muft England ftill the Scene of Changes be,
Toft and Tempeftuous like our Ambient Sea?
Muft ftill our Weather and our Wills agree?
Without our Blood our Liberties we have
Who that is Free would Fight to be a Slave?
Or what can Wars to After-times Affure,
Of which our Prefent Age is not fecure?
All that our Monarch would for us Ordain,
Is but t' Injoy the Bleffings of his Reign.
Our Land's an Eden, and the Main's our Fence,
While we preferve our State of Innocence;
That loft, then Beafts their Bruital Force imply,
And firft their Lord, and then themfelves deftroy:
What Civil Broils have coft, we know too well,
Oh let it be enough, that once we fell.
And every Heart confpire with every Tongue,
Still to have fuch a King, and this King Long.

THE
𝕌𝕟𝕙𝕒𝕡𝕡𝕪 𝔽𝕒𝕧𝕠𝕦𝕣𝕚𝕥𝕖;
OR, THE
EARL of ESSEX.

Actus Primus, Scena Prima.

Countess of Nottingham, Burleigh *at several Doors.*
The Countess reading a Letter.

Not. HELP me to rail, prodigious minded *Burleigh*,
Prince of bold *English* Councils, teach me how
This hateful Breast of mine may Dart forth words
Keen as thy Wit, Malicious as thy Person;
Then I'll caress thee, stroak thee into shape.
This Rocky dismal Form of thine that holds
The most Seraphick Mind, that ever was;
I'll heal and Mould thee with a soft Embrace;
Thy Mountain Back shall yield beneath these Arms,
And thy pale wither'd Cheeks that never glow,
Shall then be deck'd with Roses of my own——
Invent some new strange Curse that's far above
Weak Womans Rage to Blast the Man I Love.
  Burl. What means the fairest of the Court, say what
More cruel Darts are forming in those Eyes
To make Adoring *Cecil* more unhappy?
If such a Wretched, and declar'd hard Fate
Attends the Man you Love, what then, bright Star,
Has your Malignant Beauty yet in Store
For him that is the Object of your Scorn:
Tell me that most unhappy, happy Man,
Declare who is this most ungrateful Lover?
And to obey my lovely *Nottingham*
I will prefer this dear Cabal, and her
To all the other Councils in the World;

B   Nay

Nay tho' the Queen, and her two Nations call'd,
And finking *England* ftood this hour in need
For this fupporting Head, they all fhou'd fue,
Or perifh all for one kind look from you.

   Not. There fpoke the *Genius*, and the Breath of *England.*
Thou *Æfculapius* of the Chriftian World!
Methinks the Queen, in all her Majefty,
Hem'd with a Pomp of Rufty Swords, and duller Brains,
When thou art abfent, is a naked Monarch,
And fills an idle Throne till *Cecil* comes
To head her Councils, and infpire her Generals ——
Thy uncooth felf that feems a Scourge to Nature
For fo malicioufly deforming thee,
Is by the Heavenly Powers ftamp'd with a Soul
That like the Sun breaks through dark Mifts, when none
Beholds the Cloud, but Wonders at the Light.

   Burl. O fpare that Angel's Voice till the laft Day,
Such Heav'nly Praife is loft on fuch a Subject.

   Not. Let none prefume to fay, while *Burleigh* Lives,
A Woman wears the Crown; Fourth *Richard* rather,
Heir to the Third in Magnanimity,
In Perfon, Courage, Wit, and Bravery all,
But to his Vices none, nor to his End
I hope.

   Burl. You Torture me with this Excefs ——
Were but my Flefh Caft in a Purer Mould,
Then you might fee me Blufh. But my hot Blood
Burnt with Continual thought, do's inward Glow;
Thought like the Sun ftill goes its daily Round,
And Scorches, as in *India*, to the Root. ——
But to the Wretched Caufe of your difturbance;
Say, fhall I guefs? is *Effex* not the Man?

   Not. O! Name not *Effex*, Hell, and Tortures rather,
Poifons and Vultures to the Breaft of Man
Are not fo Cruel as the Name of *Effex* ——
Speak, good my Lord; nay, never fpeak nor think
Again, unlefs you can affwage this worfe
Than Fury in my Breaft.

   Burl. Tell me the Caufe.
Then ceafe your Rage, and Study to Revenge.

   Not. My Rage! It is the Wing by which I'll Fly
To be Reveng'd —— I'll ne're be Patient more.
Lift me my Rage, nay, Mount me to the Stars,
Where I may Hunt this *Peacock*, tho' he lies
Clofe in the Lap of *Juno* —— *Elizabeth*;
Tho' the Queen Circles him with Charms of Pow'r,
And hides her Minion like another *Circe*.

Or, *The Earl of* Effex.

Burl. Still well Inftructed Rage, but pray difclofe
The Reafon of the Earl's Misfortune.

Not. You are,
My Friend, the Cabinet of all my Frailties ;
From you, as from Juft Heav'n, hope for Abfolution ;
Yet pray, tho' Anger makes me Red, when I
Difcourfe the Reafon of my Rage, be kind,
And fay it is my Sex's Modefty.
Know then,
This bafe imperious Man I Lov'd, Lov'd fo,
Till Lingering with the pain of Fierce defire,
And fhame that ftrove to Torture me alike,
At laft I paft the Limits of our Sex,
And (O kind *Cecil* pity and forgive me)
Sent this opprobrious Man my Mind a Slave ;
In a kind Letter Broke the filence of
My Love, which rather fhou'd have broke my Heart.

Burl. But pray, what Anfwer did you get from him ?
Not. Such as has made an Earthquake in my Soul,
Shook ev'ry Vital in thefe tender Limbs,
And rais'd me to the Storm you found me in.
At firft he Charm'd me with a thoufand Hopes,
Elfe 'twas my Love thought all his Actions fo ——
Juft now from *Ireland* I receiv'd this Letter,
Which take and Read ; but now I think you fhall not ——
I'll tear it in a thoufand pieces firft,
Tear it, as I wou'd *Effex* with my Will,
To Bits, to Morfels, Hack the mangl'd Slave,
Till ev'ry Attome of his Curfed Body   [*Tears the Lett*
Sver'd, and Flew like Duft before the Wind.
Now do I blefs the Chance, all elfe may blame
Me for Revealing of my Foolifh Paffion ——
Did I e'er think thefe Celebrated Charms
Which I fo often have been Bleft, and Prais'd for,
Shou'd once be deftin'd to fo mean a Price,
As a Refufal ! —— Are there Friends above
That Protect Innocence, and injur'd Love ?
Hear me, and Curfe me ftreight with Wrinckl'd Age,
With Leprofie, Derifion, all your Plagues
On Earth, and Hell hereafter, if I'm not Reveng'd.

Burl. Elfe fay fhe is no Woman, or no Widow ——
The Sacred Guardians of your flighted Beauties,
Have had more Pity on their Lovely Charge,
Than to behold you fwallow'd in his Ruin.
The beft, and worft that Fortune cou'd propofe,
To you in *Effex* Love, was to have brought
A helplefs, fhort-liv'd Traitor to your Arms.

B 2

Not. Ha! Traytor, say you! Speak that Word again —
Yet do not; 'tis enough if *Burleigh* says it:
His Wit has Power to Damn the Man that thinks it,
And t'extract Treason from infected Thought.
The Nation's safety like a Ship he Steers,
When Tempests Blow, rais'd by designs of false,
And Ignorant States-men: By his Wit alone
They're all Dispers't, and by his Breath she Sails,
His Prosperous Counsel's all her gentle Gales.

Enter a Gentleman.

Gent. My Lord, the Queen expects you streight.
Burl. Madam,
Be pleas'd to Attend her Majesty i'th' *Presence*,
Where you shall hear such Misdemeanours offer'd
Such Articles against the Earl of *Essex*,
As will both glad the Nation, and your self.
Gent. My Lord I see the haughty Earl of *Southampton*
Coming this way.
Burl. Madam, retire.
Not. I go
With greater expectation of delight,
Than a young Bridegroom on his Marriage Night.   [*Exit* Countess
                                                         of *Notting.*

Burl. *Southampton*, he's the chief of *Essex* Faction,
His Friend, and Sworn Brother; and I fear
Too much a Friend, and Partner of his Revels,
To be a Stranger to the other's Guilt ———
'Tis not yet time to lop this haughty Bough,
Till I have shaken first the Tree that bears it.

Enter Southampton.

South. My Lord, I hear unwelcome News; 'tis said
Some Factious Members of the House, Headed
By you, have Voted an Address for leave
T'impeach the Earl of *Essex* of strange Articles
Of Treason.
Burl. Treason, 'tis most true is laid
To *Essex* Charge; but that I am the Cause
They do me wrong, th'Occasion is too publick;
For those dread Storms in *Ireland* rais'd by him,
Have blown so rudely on our *English* Coasts,
That they have Shipwrack'd quite the Nation's Peace,
And wak'd it's very Statues to abhorring.
South. Meer Argument, your nice, and fine distinctions,

To

Or, *The Earl of* Essex.

To make a good Man Vitious, or a bad
Man Vertuous, ev'n as pleafe the Sophifters———
My Lord, you are ingendring Snakes within you,
I fear you have a fubtile ftinging Heart;
And give me leave to tell you, that this Treafon,
f any, has been hatch'd in *Burleigh*'s School.
i fee Ambition in the fair Pretence,
Burleigh in all its Cunning, dark Difguifes,
And envious *Cecil* ev'ry where.

 Burl. My Lord, my Lord, your Zeal to this bad Earl
Makes you offend the Queen, and all good men.
Believe it, Sir, his Crimes have been fo noted,
So plain, and open to the State, and her,
That he can now no more deceive the Eyes
Of a Moft Gracious Miftrefs, or her Council;
Nor can fhe any longer, if fhe wou'd,
In pity of his other Parts, let Juftice wink,
But rouze her felf from Cheated flumbering *Mercy*,
And ftart at his moft foul Ingratitude.
Nor do's it well become the brave *Southampton*
To plead in his behalf; for fear it pulls
Upon himfelf, fufpicion of his Crimes.

 South. Hold in my Fire, and fcorch not through my Ribs,
Quench, if thou canft, the Burning furious pain ———
I cannot if I wou'd, but muft unload
Some of the Torture——Now by my wrong'd felf,
And *Effex* much more wrong'd, I fwear 'tis falfe,
Falfe as the Rules by which Vile Statefmen Govern,
Falfe as their Arts, by which the Traytors Rife,
By Cheating Nations, Deftroying Kings,
And falfe impofing on the Common Crew.
Effex! By all the Hopes of my Immortal Soul,
There's not one drop of Blood, of that brave Man
But holds more Honour, Truth and Loyalty,
Than thy whole Mafs befides, and all thy Brains
Stufft with Cabals, and Projects for the Nation;
Than thou that feem'ft a good St. *Chriftopher*
Carrying thy Country's *Genius* on thy Back,
But art indeed a Devil, and takeft more Hire
Than Half the Kingdom's Wealth can fatisfie.
I fay again, that thou, and all thy Race,
With *Effex* bafe Accufers, ev'ry one
Put in a Scale together, weigh not half
The merit that's in one poor Hair of his.

 Burl. Thank you, my Lord———fee I can bear the Scandal
And cannot chufe but fmile, to fee you Rage.

 South. It is, becaufe thy Guilty Soul's a Coward,

And has not Spirit enough to feign a Paſſion.

    Burl. It is the Token of my Innocence.——
But let *Southampton* have a ſpecial Care
To keep his cloſe Deſigns from *Cecil's* way,
Leſt he diſturb the *Genius* of the Nation,
As you were pleas'd to call me ; and beware
The Fate of *Eſſex.*   [*Exit* Burleigh.

    South. Ha*!* The Fate of *Eſſex!*
Thou lyeſt Proud Stateſman, 'tis above thy reach ;
As high above thy malice as is Heaven
Beyond a *Cecil's* Hopes —— Deſpair not *Eſſex !*
Nor his brave Friends, ſince a Juſt Queen's his Judge ;
She that ſaw once ſuch Wonders in thy Perſon,
A ſcarce fledg'd Youth, as Loading thee with Honours,
At once made thee Earl-Marſhal, Knight o'th' Garter,
Chief Counſellor, and Admiral at Sea————
She comes, ſhe comes bright Goddeſs of the Day,
And *Eſſex's* Foes ſhe drives like Miſts away.

    Enter the Queen, Burleigh, *Lord Chanceller, Counteſs of* Nottingham,
        Counteſs of Rutland. *Lords and Attendants, Queen*
            on a Chair of State, Guards.

    Queen. My Lords, we hear not any thing confirms
The New Deſigns were dreaded of the *Spaniards* :
Our Letters lately from our Agent there
Say nothing of ſuch Fears, nor do I think
They dare.

    Burl. To dare, moſt High Illuſtrious Princeſs,
Is ſuch a Virtue *Spaniard* never knew,
His Courage is as Cold as he is Hot,
And Faith is as Adulterate as his Blood.
What Truth can we expect from ſuch a Race
Of Mungrels, Jews, Mahumetans, Goths, Moors,
And Indians, with a few of Old Caſtillians,
Shuffl'd in Nature's Mould together ?
That *Spain* may truly now be call'd the Place
Where *Babel* firſt was Built.   Theſe Men
With all falſe Tenets chopt and maſht together,
Suck'd from the Scum of ev'ry baſe Religion,
Which they have ſince Transform'd to *Romiſh* Maſs,
Are now become the Mitre's darling Sons,
And *Spain* is call'd the *Pope's* moſt Catholick King.

    Queen. Spoke like true *Cecil* ſtill, Old Proteſtant——
But, Oh! it Joys me with the dear Remembrance
Of this Romantick huge Invaſion.
From the *Pope's* Cloſet where 'twas firſt Begot,

                                    Bulls

Or, *The Earl of* Essex.

Bulls, Abfolutions, Pardons, frightful Banns,
Flew o'er the Continent, and Narrow Seas,
Some to Reward, and others to Torment,
Nay, worfe, Inquifition was let loofe
To teach the very Atheifts Purgatory.
Then were a Thoufand Holy hands employ'd,
As Cardinals, Bifhops, Abbots, Monks, and Jefuites,
Not a poor Mendicant, or Begging Friar,
But thought he fhou'd be Damn'd to leave the Work.
  South Whole Sholes of Benedictions were difperft ;
Nay, the good *Pope* himfelf fo weary'd was
With giving Bleffings to thefe Holy Warriours,
That Flew to him, from ev'ry Part as thick
As Hornets to their Neft, it gave his Arms
The Gout.
  Burl. O Faithlefs, incouragious Hands!
They fhou'd have both been burnt for Hereticks.
  Queen. But when this huge, and mighty Fleet was ready
Altars were ftrip'd of fhining Ornaments :
Their Images, their Pictures, Palls, and Hangings,
By Nuns, and Perfians wrought,
All went to help their great Armada forth ;
Relicks of all degrees of Saints
Were there diftributed, and not a Ship
Was Bleft without one ; ev'ry Sail amongft 'em
Boafted to carry, as a certain Pledge
Of Victory, fome of the real Crofs.
  South. Long live that Day, and never be forgotten
The gallant Hour when to th' immortal Fame
Of *England*, and the more immortal *Drake*,
That Proud Armado was deftroy'd ; yet was
The Fight not half fo dreadful as th' Event
Was pleafant When the firft broad-fides were giv'n,
A tall brave Ship, the talleft of the Reft,
That feem'd the Pride of all their big Halfmoon,
Whether by Chance, or by a lucky Shot
From us, I know not, but fhe was Blown up,
Burfting like Thunder, and almoft as high,
And then did fhiver in a Thoufand Pieces,
Whilft from her Belly Crouds of Living Creatures
Broke like untimely Births, and fill'd the Sky.
Then might be feen a *Spaniard* catch his Fellow,
And wreftling in the Air fall down together ;
A Prieft for Safety rifing on a Crofs,
Another that had none, croffing himfelf ;
Frias with long big fleeves like Magpies Wings
That bore them up, came Gently Sailing down :

One with a Don that held him by the Arms,
And cry'd, Confess me straight; but as he just
Had spoke the Words, they Tumbl'd down together.

Burl. Just Heav'n that never ceas'd to have a Care
Of your most Gracious Majesty and Kingdoms,
By Valiant Souldiers, and by Faithful Leaders,
Confounded in one day the vast Designs
Of *Italy*, and *Spain* against our Liberties;
So may *Tyrone*, and *Irish* Rebels fall,
And so may all your Captains henceforth prove
To be as Loyal, and as stout Commanders.

Queen. Is there no fresher News from *Ireland* yet?

Burl. None better than the last, that seems too ill
To be repeated in your Gracious hearing.

Queen. Why, What was that?

South. Now, now the subtil Fiend   } *Aside.*
Begins to Conjure up a Storm.

Burl. How soon your Gracious Majesty forgets
Crimes done by any of your Subjects!

Queen. What?
That *Essex* did defer his Journey to
The North, and therefore lost the Season quite;
Was not that all?

Burl. And that he met *Tyrone*
At his Request, and treated with him private.
A Ford dividing them, they both Rode in,
Wading their Horses Knee deep on each side;
But that the Distance from each other was
So great, and they were forc'd to parly loud,
Orders were given to keep the Soldiers off;
Nay not an Officer in all the Army
But was deny'd to hear what pass'd between them———
What follow'd then the Parly? was the Truce,
So shameful, (if I may be bold to call
It so,) both to your Majesty and *England*?

Queen. Enough, enough, good *Cecil*, you begin
To be inveterate; 'Twas his first fault;
And tho' that Crime's done to th' Nation's hurt
Admit of no Excuse or Mitigation
From th' Author's many Virtues or Misfortunes,
Yet you must all confess that he is brave,
Valiant as any, and 'as done as much
For you as e'er *Alcides* did for *Greece*.
Yet I'll not hide his Faults, but blame him too,
And therefore I have sent him Chiding Letters,
Forbidding him to leave the Kingdom, till
He has dispatcht the War, and kill'd *Tyrone*.

*Enter Sir Walter Rawleigh, Attended by some
other Members of the House.*

Burl. Most Royal Madam, here's the gallant *Rawleigh,*
With others in Commission from the House,
Who attended your Majesty with some few Bills
And humblest of Addresses, that you wou'd
Be pleas'd to pass 'em for the Nation's safety.

Queen. Welcome my People, welcome to your Queen,
Who wishes still no longer to be so
Than she can Govern well, and serve you all;
Welcome again, dear People; for I'm Proud
To call you so; and let it not be boasting
In me to say I love you with a greater Love
Than ever Kings before showr'd down on Subjects,
And that I think ne'er did a People more
Deserve, than you. Be quick
And tell me your Demands; I long to hear:
For know, I count your wants are all my own.

Rawl. Long live the bright Imperial Majesty
Of *England,* Virgin Star of Christendom,
Blessing, and Guide of all your Subjects, Lives,
Who with the Sun may sooner be extinguish'd
From the bright Orb he Rules in, than their Queen
Shou'd e'er descend the Throne she now makes happy.
Your Parliament, most blest of Sovereigns,
Calling to mind the Providence of Heaven
In Guarding still your People under you,
And sparing your most Precious Life,
Do humbly offer to your Royal Pleasure
Three Bills to be made Living Acts hereafter,
All for the safety of your Crown and Life,
More precious than ten thousand of your Slaves.

Queen. Let *Cecil* take and read what they contain.

Burl. An Act for settling and establishing   [*Cecil* takes the Papers,
A Strong Militia out of every County.   and reads the Contents.
And likewise for levying a new Army
Consisting of sixt thousand Foot at least,
And Horse three thousand, quickly to be ready,
As a strong Guard for the Queen's Sacred Person,
And to prevent what clandestine Designs
The Spaniards, or the Scots may have.

Queen. Thanks to
My Dear, and loving People; I will pass it.

Burl. This Second Act is for the speedy raising
Two Hundred Thousand Pounds to pay the Army

C   And

And to be ordered as the Queen shall please;
This to be gathered by a Benevolence,
And Subsidy, in six Months time from hence.
 Queen. What mean my giving Subjects! it shall pass.
 Burl. The third has several Articles at large
With an Address subscrib'd, most humbly offer'd
For the Impeaching *Robert* Earl of *Essex*
Of several Misdemeanors of High-Treason.
 Queen. Ha!
This unthought blast has shockt me like an Ague——⎫
It has alarm'd every Sense, and spoil'd me   ⎬*Aside.*
Of all the Awful Courage of a Queen;   ⎭
But I'll recover——Say, my *Nottingham*,
And *Rutland*, did you ever hear the like!
But are you well assur'd I am awake?
Bless me and say it is a horrid Vision,
That I am not upon the Throne————
Ha! Is't not so?——Yes, Traytors, I'll obey you————
           [*She rises in a Rage.*

Here sit you in my place; take *Burleigh*'s Staff,
The Chancellor's Seal and *Essex*'s valiant Head,
And leave me none but such as are your selves,
Knaves for my Counsel, Fools for Magistrates,
And Cowards for Commanders————Oh my Heart!
 South. O horrid imposition on a Throne!
Essex; that has so bravely serv'd the Nation!
That I may boldly say, *Drake* did not more,
That has so often beat his Foes on Land,
Stood like a Promontory in its defence,
And Sail'd with Dragons Wings to Guard the Seas;
Essex! That took as many Towns in *Spain*
As all this Island hold, begger'd their Fleet
That came with Loads of half their Mines in *India*,
And took a mighty Carrack of such Value,
That held more Gold in its Prodigious Deck
Than serv'd the Nation's Riot in a Year.
 Queen. Ingrateful People! Take away my Life;
'Tis that you'd have: For I have Reign'd too long————
You too well know that I'm a Woman, else
You durst not use me thus————had you but fear'd
Your Queen as you did once my Royal Father,
Or had I but the Spirit of that Monarch,
With one short Syllable I shou'd have ram'd
Your impudent Petitions down your Throats,
And made Four hundred of your Factious Crew
Tremble, and grovel on the Earth for fear.

              Rawl.

Rawl. Thus proftrate at your Feet we beg for Pardon,
And humbly crave your Majefties Forgivenefs.   [*Petitioners kneel.*
    Queen. No more——Attend me in the Houfe to morrow.
    Burl. Moft Mighty Queen! Bleft and Ador'd by all,
Torment not fo your Royal Breaft with Paffion :
Not all of us, our Lives, Eftates and Country
Are worth the leaft difturbance of your Mind.
    Queen. Are you become a Pleader for fuch Traytors!
Ha! I fufpect that *Cecil* too is envious,
And *Effex* is too great for thee to grow——,
A Shrub that never fhall be look'd upon,
Whilft *Effex* that's a Cedar ftands fo nigh——
Tell me, why was not I acquainted with
This clofe Defign : For I am fure thou know'ft it.
    Burl. Madam——
    Queen. Be dumb; I will hear no Excufes——
I could turn Cynick, and outrage the Wind,
Fly from all Courts, from Bufinefs, and Mankind,
Leave all like *Chaos* in Confufion hurl'd :
For 'tis not Reafon now that rules the World :
There's Order in all States but Man below,
And all things elfe do to Superiours bow ;
Trees, Plants, and Fruits, rejoyce beneath the Sun,
Rivers, and Seas are guided by the Moon ;
The Lyon rules through Shades and ev'ry Green,
And Fifhes own the Dolphin for their Queen ;
But Man, the verier Monfter, worfhips ftill
No God but Luft, no Monarch but his Will.

                                        [*Exeunt omnes.*

Finis Actus Primi.

Actus Secundus, Scena prima.

Countefs of Effex.

C. *Eff.* **I**S this the joy of a new Marry'd Life?
      This all the Taft of Pleafures that are Feign'd
      To flow from fweet and Everlafting Springs?
      By what falfe Opticks do we view thofe fights,
And by our ravenous Wifhes feem to draw
Delights fo far beyond a Mortals reach,
And bring 'em home to our deluded Breafts?
'Tis not yet long fince that bleft Day was paft,
A Day I wifh that fhou'd for ever laft;
                    C 2   The

The Night once gone, I did the Morning-chide,
Whose Beams betray'd me by my *Essex* side;
And whil'st my Blushes, and my Eyes they blest,
I strove to hide 'em in his panting Breast,
And my hot Cheeks close to his Bosom laid,
Listning to what the Guest within it said;
Were Fire to Fire the Noble heart did burn,
Close like a Phœnix in her spicy Urn:
I sigh'd, and wept for Joy, a shower of Tears,
And felt a thousand sweet and pleasant fears,
Too rare for Sense, too exquisite to say ;
Pain we can count, but Pleasure steals away :
But business now, and envious Glory's Charms,
Have snatch't him from these ever Faithful Arms:
Ambition, that's the highest way to Woe,
Cruel Ambition! Love's Eternal Foe.

Enter Southampton.

South. Thou dearest Partner of my dearest Friend,
The brightest Planet of thy Shining Sex,
Forgive me for the unwelcome News I bring, ——
Essex is come the most deplor'd of Men !
    C. *Ess.* Now by the Sacred Joys that fills my heart,
What fatal meaning can there be in that ?
Is my Lord come ? say, speak.
    South. Too sure he's come ———
But oh that Seas, as wide as Waters flow,
Or burning Lakes as broad and deep as Hell,
Had rather parted you for ever,
So *Essex* had been safe on th' other side.
    C. *Ess.* My Lord, You much amaze me ———
Pray what of ill has happen'd since this Morning,
That the Queen Guarded him with so much mercy,
And then refus'd to hear his false impeachers ?
    South. Too soon, alas ! h'as forfeited his Honours,
Places and Wealth, but more his precious Life;
Condemn'd by the too cruel Nation's Laws,
For leaving his Commission, and returning,
When the Queen's Absolute Commands forbid him.
    C. *Ess.* Fond hopes ! must then our meeting prove so fatal
    South. Say, Madam, now what help will you purpose,
Can the Queen's Pity any more protect him?
Never, it is no longer in her Power,
She must tho' 'gainst her will deliver him
A Sacrifice to all his greedy Foes.
    C. *Ess.* Where is my Lord ?

South. Blunt left him on the Way,
And came disguis'd in haste to give me notice.

C. *Ess.* Let him go back; and give my *Essex* warning,
Conjuring him from us to stir no further,
But straight return to *Ireland* e're 'tis known
He left the Place.

South. Alas is is no secret;
Besides, he left the Town almost as soon
As *Blunt*, and is expected every moment.

C. *Ess.* How cou'd it be reveal'd so suddenly?

South. I know not that, unless from Hell it came,
Where *Cecil* too is Privy Counsellor,
And knows as much as any Devil there:
I met the Cunning Fiend and *Rawleigh* whispering;
And the fair Treacherous *Nottingham*;
I saw bedeck'd with an ill-natur'd smile
That shew'd malicious Beauty to the height.

C. *Ess.* Hold, hold, my Lord, my fears begin to wrack me,
And Danger now in all it's horrid Shapes,
Stalks in my way; and makes my Blood run cold,
Worse than a thousand Glaring Spirits cou'd do.
Assist me straight thou *Damon* to my *Essex*,
Help me thou more than Friend in Misery
I'll to the Queen; and streight declare our Marriage;
She will have mercy on my helpless State,
Pity these Tears, and all my humble Postures;
If not for me, nor for my *Essex* sake;
Yet for the Illustrious Off-spring that I bear;
I'll go, I'll run, I'll hazard all this Moment. [*Offers to be gone.*]

South. Led by vain Hopes, you fly to your Destruction;
There wants but that dread Secret to be known,
To tumble you for ever to Despair,
And leave you both Condemn'd without the Hopes
Of the Queen's Pity, or Remorse hereafter.

C. *Ess.* Curst be the Stars that flatter'd at our Births,
That shone so bright, with such unusual Lustre,
As cheated the whole World into belief
Our Lives alone were all the chiefest Care.

South. Be Comforted, rely on *Essex*'s Fate,
And the Queen's Mercy ——
Behold she comes, our evil Fate,
In discontented Characters wrote on
Her Brow.

Enter the Queen, Burleigh, *Countess of* Nottingham,
Rawleigh, *Attendant Guards.*

Queen. Is *Essex* then Arriv'd?
Burl. He is.
Queen. Then he has loft me all the flattering Hopes   〔*Aside.*
I ever had to fave him————Come, fay you!
Who elfe came with him ?
   Burl. Some few Attendants.
   Queen. Durft the moft vile of Traytors ferve me thus !
Double my ftrength about me, draw out Men,
And fet a Guard before the Palace Gates,
And bid my valiant Friends the Citizens
Be ready ftraight————I fhall be murder'd elfe,
And faithful *Cecil*, If thou lov'ft thy Queen,
See all this done : For how can I be fafe,
If *Essex* that I favour'd, feeks my Life.
   Burl. Will't pleafe your Majefty to fee the Earl?
   Queen. No.
   Burl. Shall I publifh ftraight your Royal Order,
That may forbid his coming to the Court,
Until your Majefty command him ?
   Queen. Neither————
How durft you feem t'interpret what's my Pleafure?
No, I will fee him if a' comes, and then
Leave me to act without your faucy Aid,
If I have any Royal Power.
   C. Eff. Bleft be the Queen, bleft be the pitying God   〔*Aside.*
That has Infpir'd her.
   South. Moft admir'd of Queen's
Thus low unto the ground I bend my Body,
And wifh I cou'd fink lower through the Earth,
To fuit a pofture to my humble Heart.
I tremble to excufe my gallant Friend
In contradiction to your Heavenly Will ;
Who like a God knows all, and 'tis enough
You think him innocent, and he is fo ;
But yet your Majefty's moft Royal Soul,
That foars fo high above the humble Malice
Of bafe and fordid Wretches under you,
Perhaps is Ignorant the valiant Earl
Has Foes, Foes that are only fo, becaufe
Your Majefty has Crown'd him with your Favours,
And lifted him fo far above their fights.
That 'tis a pain to all their envious Eyes
To look fo high above him ; and of thefe

Some

Some grow too near your Royal Perfon,
As the ill Angels did at firft in Heaven,
And daily feek to hurt this brave Man's Virtue.

Queen. Help me thou infinite Ruler of all things,
That fees at once far as the Sun difplays,
And fearches every Soul of human kind,
Quick, and unfelt, as Light infufes Beams,
Unites, and makes all Contradictions centre,
And to the fence of Man, which is more ftrange,
Governs innumerable diftant Parts
By one intire fame Providence at once.
Teach me fo far thy Holy Art of Rule,
As in a mortal reafon may diftinguifh
Betwixt bold Subjects, and a Monarch's Right.

Burl. May't pleafe your Majefty, the Earl is come,
And waits your Pleafure.

Queen. Let him be admitted————
Now, now fupport thy Royalty,
And hold thy Greatnefs firm; but oh how heavy
A Load is State where the Free Mind's difturb'd?
How happy a Maid is fhe that always Lives
Far from high Honour, in a low content,
Where neither Hills, nor dreadful Mountains grow,
But in a Vale where Springs and Pleafures flow;
Where Sheep lye round inftead of Subjects Throngs,
The Trees for Mufick, Birds inftead of Songs;
Inftead of *Effex* one Poor faithful Hind,
He as a Servant, She a Miftrefs kind,
Who with Garlands for her coming Crowns her Door,
And all with Rufhes ftrews her little Floor:
Where at their mean Repaft no Fears attend
Of a Falfe Enemy, or a falfer Friend;
No care of Scepters, nor Ambitious Frights
Difturb the quiet of their fleep at Nights————
He comes; this proud Invader of my Reft,
A' comes: But I intend fo to receive him————

Enter the Earl of Effex *with Attendants.*

Effex kneels. The Queen *turns to the* Countefs *of* Nottingham.
Effex. Long live the mightieft, moft ador'd of Queens,
The brighteft Power on Earth that Heav'n e'er form'd;
Aw'd and amaz'd the trembling *Effex* kneels,
Effex that ftood the dreadful voice of Cannons,
Hid in a darker Field of Smoak and Fire,
Than that where Cyclops blows the Forge, and fweats
Beneath the mighty Hill, whilft Bullets round me

Flew

Flow like the Boks of Heav'n when shot with Thunder,
And dost their Fury on my Shield and Corslet;
And stood those Dangers unconcern'd, and dauntless;
But your most Majestiek brightest Form
That ever Rul'd on Earth, have caught my Soul,
Surpriz'd its Vertues all with dread and wonder;
My humble Eyes durst scarcely look up to you,
Your dazling Mien, and Sight so fill the place,
And every Part Celestial Rays adorn.

   Queen. Ha!   [*Aside.*

   Essex. 'Tis said I have been guilty——
I dare not rise, but crawl thus on the Earth,
'Till I have leave to kiss your Sacred Robe,
And clear before the justest, best of Queens,
My wrong'd and wounded Innocence.

   Queen. What said'st thou *Nottingham?* what said the Earl? [*Aside.*

   Essex. What not a Word! a Look! not one blest Look!
Turn, turn your cruel Brow, and kill me with
A Frown; it is a quick and surer way
To rid you of your *Essex,*
Than Banishment, Than Fetters, Swords, or Axes——
What not that neither! Then I plainly see
My Fate, the Malice of Enemies
Triumphant in their joyful Faces; *Burleigh*
With a glad Coward's Smile, that knows h'as got
Advantage o'er his valiant Foe, and *Rawleigh's* proud
To see his dreaded *Essex* kneel so long,
Essex that stood in his great Mistress Favour
Like a huge Oak, the loftiest of the Wood,
Whilst they no higher cou'd attain to be
Than humble Succours nourisht by my Root,
And like the Ivy twin'd their flatt'ring Arms
About my Waste, and liv'd but by my Smiles——

   Queen. I must be gone: For if I stay I shall
Here wrack my Conduct, and my Fame for ever——
Thus the Charm'd Pilot list'ning to the Syrens,
Lets his rich Vessel split upon a Rock,
And loses both his Life and Wealth together.   }[*Aside.*

   Essex. Still am I shun'd as if I were destruction——   [*Rises.*
Here, here, my faithful and my vailant Friends,
Dearest Companions of the Fate of *Essex,*
Behold this bosom studded o'er with Scars,
This marble breast, that has so often held,
Like a fierce Battlement against the Foes
Of *England's* Queen, that made a hundred breaches;
Here pierce it straight, and through this Wild of Wounds
Be sure to reach my Heart, this Loyal Heart,

                       Th..

That fits confulting 'midft a thoufand Spirits
All at command, all faithful to my Queen.

Queen. If I had ever Courage, Haughtinefs,
Or Spirit, help me but now, and I am happy! ⎫
He melts; it flows, and drowns my Heart with Pity, ⎬ *Afide.*
If I ftay longer I fhall tell him fo——— ⎭
What is this Traytor in my fight!
All that have Loyalty, and love their Queen,
Forfake this horrid Wretch, and follow me.

Exeunt *Queen and her Attendants,* manet *Effex* folus

Effex. She's gone, and darted fury as fhe went——
Cruelleft of Queens!
Not heard! Not hear your Souldier fpeak one word!
Effex that once was all day liften'd to;
Effex, that like a Cherub held thy Throne,
Whilft thou didft drefs me with thy wealthy Favours,
Cheer'd me with Smiles, and deck'd me round with Glories;
Nor was thy Crown fcarce worfhip'd on thy head
Without me by thy Side; but now art deaf
As Adders, Winds, or the remorfelefs Seas,
Deaf as thy cunning Sex's Ears to thofe
That make unwelcome Love——What News my Friend?

Enter Southampton.

South. Such as I dare not tell; but pardon me,
As an Ill Bird that perches on the fide
Of fome tall Ship foretels a ftorm at hand,
I come to give you warning of the danger———
See *Cecil* with a Meffage from the Queen.

Eff. Then does my Wrack come rouling on apace;
That foul Leviathan ne'er yet appear'd
Without a horrid Tempeft from his Noftrils.

Enter to them Burleigh and Rawleigh.

Burl. Hear *Robert* Earl of *Effex,*
Hear what the Queen, my Lord, by us pronounces;
She now divefts you of your Offices,
Your Dignities of Governour of *Ireland,*
Earl Martial, Mafter of her Horfe, General
Of all her Forces both by Land and Sea,
And Lord Lieutenant of the feveral Counties,
Of *Effex, Hereford,* and *Weftmorland.*

Eff. A vaft and goodly fumm all at one Caft
By an unlucky hand thrown quite away.

D

Burl. Alſo her pleaſure is, that in obedience
To her Commands, you ſend your Staff by us,
Then leave the Court, and ſtir no farther than
Your Houſe, till order from the Queen and Council.

Eſſ. Thanks my Misfortunes, for you fall with weight
Upon me, and Fate ſhoots her Arrows thick;
'Tis hard if they find not one mortal Place
About me———

Burl. My Lord, what ſhall we tell her Majeſty?
What is your Anſwer, for the Queen expects us?

Eſſ. Wilt thou then promiſe to be juſt, and tell her?
Give her a Caution of her worſt of Foes,
Thy greedy ſelf, the Land's infeſting Giant,
Exacting Heads from her beſt Subjects daily;
Worſe than the *Phrygian* Monſter, he was more
Cheaply compounded with, and but devour'd
Sev'n Virgins in a Week, and ſpar'd the reſt.

South. Hold, my brave Friend, waſt not the Noble Breath
Of *Eſſex* on ſo baſe and mean a Subject———
Thou Traytor to thy Sovereign and her Kingdoms,
More full of Guilt than e'er thou did'ſt deviſe
To lay on *Eſſex*, whom thou fear'ſt and hateſt;
And thou, becauſe thy ſordid Soul, and Perſon
Ne'er fitted thee
For gallant Actions, thinkeſt the World ſo too:
For he that looks through a foul Glaſs that's ſtain'd,
Sees all things ſtain'd like the foul Perſpective he uſes.
'Tis Crime enough in any to be valiant,
To win a Battel or be Fortunate,
Whil'ſt thou ſtand'ſt by the Queen to intercept,
Or elſe determine Favours from her Hands;
'Tis not who is too blame, or who deſerves,
Nor whom the Queen wou'd look on with a Grace,
But whom proud *Cecil* pleaſes to reward,
Or puniſh, and the Valiant never ſcape thee;
Curſt be the brave that fall into ſuch Hands;
For Cowards ſtill are cruel and malicious.

Burl. This I dare tell, and that *Southampton* ſaid it.

South. And put her too in Mind of thy vain Glories,
Such Impudence and Oſtentation in thee,
And ſo much Horrid Pride and Coſtlineſs,
As wou'd undoe a Monarch to ſupply.

Eſſ. So thrives the lazy Gown, and ſuch as Sleep
On Woolſacks, and on Seats of Injur'd Juſtice,
Or learn to prate at Council-Tables; but
How miſerable is Fortune to the Valiant!
Were but Commanders half ſo well rewarded

For all their Winters Camps, and Summers Fights,
Then they might eat, and the poor Soldiers Widows,
And Children too might all be kept from ftarving.

Raw. My Lord, in fpeaking thus you tax the Queen
Of Weaknefs and Injuftice both, and that
She favours none but worthlefs Perfons.

Burl. Muft we return this ftubborn Anfwer to her?
You'll not obey her Majefty, nor here
Refign your Staff of Offices to us?

Eff. Tell her what e'er thy Malice can invent;
Yet if thou fay'ft I'll not obey the Queen,
I tell thee, Lord,
'Tis falfe, falfe as thy moft inveterate Soul
That looks through the foul Prifon of thy Body,
And curfes all fhe fees at liberty———
I tell thee, creeping thing, the Queen's too good,
More merciful than to condemn a Slave,
Much lefs her *Effex* without hearing him———
I will appeal to her———————

Burl. You'll not believe us,
Nor that it was by her Command we came.

Effex. I do not.

Burl. Fare you well, my Lords.   [*Exeunt* Burleigh *and* Rawleigh.

Eff. Go thou
My brave *Southampton*, follow to the Queen,
And quickly e're my cruel Foes are heard,
Tell her that thus her faithful *Effex* fays,
This Star fhe decked me with; and all thefe Honours elfe,
In one bleft hour, when fcarce my tender years
Had reach'd the Age of Man, fhe heap'd upon me,
As if the Sun that fows the Seeds of Gemms
And golden Mines had fhowr'd upon my head,
And dreft me like the Bridegroom of her Favour.
This thou beheldft, and Nations wonder'd at:
The World had not a Favourite fo great,
So lov'd as I.

South. And I am witnefs too
How many gracious Smiles fhe bleft 'em with,
And parted with a Look with every Favour,
Was doubly worth the Gift, whilft the whole Court
Was fo well pleas'd, and fhew'd their wondrous Joy
In fhouting louder than the *Roman* Bands
When *Julius* and *Auguftus* were made Confuls.

Eff. Thou canft remember too, for all fhe faid was fignal,
That at the happy time fhe did inveft
Her *Effex* with this Robe of fhining Glories,
She bad me prize 'em as I wou'd my Life.

Defend

Defend 'em as I wou'd her Crown and Perfon :
Then a Rich Sword fhe put into my Hand,
And wifh'd me *Cæfar's* Fortune ; fo fhe grac'd me.

   South. So young *Alcides* , when he firft wore Arms,
Did fly to kill the *Eremanthean* Boar,
And fo *Achilles*, firft by *Thætis* made
Immortal, hafted to the Siege of *Troy*.

   Eff. Go thou *Southampton* ; for thou art my Friend,
And fuch a Friend's an Angel in diftrefs ;
Now the falfe Globe that flatter'd me is gone,
Thou art to me more Wealth, more Recompence
Than all the World was then———Intreat the   Queen
To blefs me with a Moment's fight,
And I will lay her Reliques humbly down,
As Travelling Pilgrims do before the Shrines
Of Saints they went a thoufand Leagues to vifit,
And her bright Virgin Honours all untainted,
Her Sword not fpoil'd with ruft, but wet with Blood,
All Nations Blood that difobey'd my Queen ;
This Staff that difciplin'd her Kingdoms once,
And Triumph'd o'er an hundred Victories ;
And if fhe will be pleas'd to take it, fay
My Life, the Life of once her darling *Effex*.

   South. I fly , my Lord, and let your hopes repofe
On the kind Zeal *Southampton* has to ferve you.   [*Exit* Southampton.

   Eff. Where art thou *Effex !* where are now thy Glories!
Thy Summers Garlands, and thy Winters Lawrels,
The Early Songs that ev'ry Morning wak'd thee ;
Thy Halls, and Chambers throng'd with Multitudes,
More than the Temples of the *Perfian* God,
To worfhip thy uprifing , and when I appear'd,
The Blufhing Emprefs of the Eaft, *Aurora*,
Gladded the World not half fo much as I :
Yefterday's Sun faw his great Rival thus,
The fpiteful Plannet faw me thus ador'd,
And fome tall-built Pyramid whofe height
And Golden top confronts him in his fky,
He tumbles down with Lightning in his Rage ;
So on a fudden has he fnatch'd my Garlands,
And with a Cloud impal'd my Gaudy Head,
Struck me with Thunder, dafht me from the Heavens,
And oh ! 'tis Dooms-day now, and darknefs all with me,
Here I'll lie down———Earth will receive her Son.
Take Pattern all by me, you that hunt Glory,
You that do Climb the Rounds of high Ambition ;
Yet, when y'ave reach'd, and mounted to the top,
Here you muft come by juft Degrees at laft,

If not fall headlong down at once like me——————
Here I'll abide close to my loving Centre:
For here I'm sure that I can fall no further————

Enter the Countess of Rutland.

Ha *!* what makes thou here *?* Tell me, fairest Creature;
Why art thou so in love with Misery
To come to be infected with my Woe,
And disobey the angry Queen for me *?*

C. *Ess.* Bless me, my Angel, guard me from such Sounds;
Is this the Language of a welcome Husband *!*
Are these fit words for *Essex* Bride to hear *!*
Bride I may truly call my self, for Love
Had scarce bestow'd the Blessing of one Night,
But snatch'd thee from these Arms.

Ess. My Soul *!* My Love!
Come to my Breast thou purest Excellence,
And throw thy lovely Arms about my Neck,
More soft, more sweet, more loving than the Vine.
Oh *!* I'm o're come with Joy, and sink beneath   [*They*
Thy Breast.

C. *Ess.* Take me along with thee, my Dear——————
My *Essex,* wake my Love, I say:
I am grown jealous of each Bliss without thee;
There's not a Dream, an Extasie or Joy,
But I will double in thy ravish'd Senses.
Come let's prepare, and mingle Souls together,
Thou shalt lose nothing, but a Gainer be.
Mine is as full of Love as thine can be.

Ess. Where have I been *!* but yet I have thee still——
Come sit thee down upon this humble Floor,
It was the first kind Throne that Love e'er had.
Thus like the first bright Couple let's embrace,
And fansie all around is Paradise.
It must be so; for all is Paradise
Where thou remainest, thou lovelier far than *Eve.*

C. *Ess.* And thou more brave, and nobler Person far,
Than the first Man, whom Heav'n's peculiar Care
Made for a Pattern for ingenious Nature,
Which ne'er till thee excell'd th' Original.

Ess. Thus when th' Almighty form'd the lovely Maid,
And sent her to the Bower where *Adam* lay,
The first of Men awak'd, and starting from
His mossy flow'ry Bed whereon he slept,
Lifted his eyes, and saw the Virgin coming;
Saw the bright Maid that glitter'd like a star,
Stars he had seen, but ne'er saw one so fair.

Thus they did meet, and thus they did embrace,
Thus in the infancy of pure defire,
E're Luſt, Diſpleaſures, Jealouſies, and Fears
Debauch'd the World, and plagu'd the Breaſt of Man;
Thus in the dawn of Golden Time, when Love,
And only Love, taught Lovers what to do.

   C. Eſſ. O thou moſt dear, moſt priz'd of all Mankind,
I burn, I faint, I'm raviſh'd with thy Love;
The Fever is too hot,
It ſcorches, Flames like pure Æthærial Fire,
And 'tis not Fleſh and Blood, but Spirits can bear it,
And thoſe the brighteſt of Angelick Forms.

   Eſſ. That is thy ſelf, thy only ſelf, thou faireſt;
There's not in Heav'n ſo bright a Cherubim;
No Angel there but for thy Love wou'd die;
The Thrones are all leſs happy there than I.

   C. Eſſ. O my beſt Lord! the Queen, the Queen, my Love
Ah! what have we committed to undo us!
The Pow'rs are angry, and have ſent the Queen,
The jealous Queen of all our Innocent Joys,
To drive us from our Paradiſe of Love;
And oh, my Lord! ſhe will not ere't be long
Allow us this poor Plat, this Ground to mourn on.

   Eſſ. Weep not my Soul, my Love, my infinite All——
Ah! what cou'd I expreſs if there were words
To tell how much, how tenderly my thoughts
Adore thee———Ah! theſe Tears are drops of Blood,
Thy *Eſſex* Blood, my World, my Heav'n, my Bride———
I, there's the Start of all my Joys beſide,
Bleſt that I am, that I can call thee Wiſe,
That Loves ſo well, and is ſo well belov'd.

   C. Eſſ. Ah! hold my Lord, what ſhall I ſay of you,
That beſt deſerves a Love ſo well you ſpeak of?

   Eſſ. Again thou weepeſt———By Heav'n there's not a Tear
But weighs more than the Wealth of *England*'s Crown,
O thou bright Storer of all Virtues, were there
But ſo much Goodneſs in thy Sex beſide,
It were enough to ſave all Womankind,
And keep 'em from Damnation——Still thou weepeſt——
Come let me kiſs thy Eyes, and catch thoſe Pearls,
Hold thy Cheeks cloſe to mine that none may fall,
And ſpare me ſome of theſe Celeſtial drops.
Thus as two Turtles driven by a Storm,
Drooping and weary, ſhelter'd on a Bough,
Begin to join their Malancholly voices,
Then thus they bill, and thus renew their Joys,

With quiv'ring Wings, and Cooing Notes repeat
Their Loves, and thus like us bemoan each other.

Enter a Lady.

Lady. Madam, the Queen expects you inftantly.

C. Eff. Ah what wou'd wifh to be of human kind!
Man in his Life fcarce finds a Moment's blifs,
But counts a thoufand Pains for one fhort Pleafure,
And when that comes 'tis fnatch'd away like ours.

Eff. Go my beft hopes, obey the cruel Queen———
I had forgot; thy Love, thy Beauties charm'd me,
Dearer than *Albion* to the Sailor's fight
Whom many years bar'd from his Native Country;
Looking on thee, I gaz'd my Soul away,
And quite forgot the dangerous Wrecks below———
Farewell———Nay then thou't foften me to Fondnefs———
The Queen may change, and we may meet again.

C. Eff. Farewell.

Eff. So have I feen a tall rich Ship of *India*
Of mighty Bulk teeming with golden Oar,
With profperous Gales come failing nigh the fhoar;
Her Train of Pendants born up by the Wind;
The gladfome Seas proud of the lovely Weight,
Now lift her up above the Sky in hight,
And then as foon th' officious Waves divide,
Hug the gay Thing and clafp her like a Bride,
Whilft Fifhes play, and Dolphins gather round,
And *Trytons* with their Coral Trumpets found;
Till on a hidden Rock at laft fhe's born,
Swift as our Fate, and thus in pieces torn.

[*Exeunt* feverally.

Finis Actus Secundi.

Actus Tertius. Scena Prima.

Countefs of Nottingham, Burleigh.

Not. NOW famous *Cecil*, *England* owes to thee
More than *Rome*'s State did once to *Cicero* pay;
That crufht the vaft Defigns of *Catiline*.
But what did he? Quell'd but a petty Conful,
And fav'd a Commonwealth; but thou'aft done more,
Pull'd down a haughtier far than *Catiline*,

The

Thy Nation sole Dictator for Twelve years,
And sav'd a Queen and Kingdoms by thy Wisdom.
 Burl. But what the *Roman* Senate then allow'd,
Nay and proud *Cicero* himself to *Fulvia*;
Fulvia the lovely Saver of her Country,
Must all and more be now ascrib'd to you,
To the sole Wit of beauteous *Nottingham*;
But I will cease and let the Nation praise thee,
And fix thy Statue high, as was *Minerva's*,
The great *Paladium* that Protected *Illium* —————
I came t'attend the Queen, where is she gone?
 Not. She went to her Closet, were She's now alone.
As she past by, I saw her Lovely Eyes
Clouded in sorrow, and before she spy'd me,
Sad Murmurs Eccho'd from her troubled Breast,
And straight some Tears follow'd the mournful Sound,
Which when she did perceive me, she'd have hid,
And with a piteous Sigh she strove to wipe
The drops away, but with her haste she left
Some sad remains upon her dewy Cheeks.
 Burl. What should the reason be!
 Not. At *Essex* Answer.
 Burl. What said she then?
No doubt th' Affront had stung her!
But kind *Southampton*, faithful to his Friend
In all things, came, and with a cunning Tale,
Which she too willingly inclin'd to hear,
Turn'd her to mildness, and at his Request,
Promis'd to see the Earl, and hear him speak
To Vindicate his Crimes, which bold *Southampton*
Declar'd to be his Enemies Aspersions;
And now is *Essex* sent for to the Court.
 Not. Then I am lost, and my designs unravell'd.
If once she sees him, all's undone again——— ———
 Burl. Behold the Closet opens —— see the Queen———
'Tis Dangerous to interrupt her——— let's Retire.
 Not. Be you not seen; I'll wait within her call.

  Enter the Queen alone, as from her Closet.   Exit *Burleigh*

 Queen. Where am I now? Why wander I alone?
What drags my Body forth without a Mind,
In all things like a Statue, but in Mothon?
There's Something I would say, but know not what,
Nor yet to whom——O wretched State of Princes!
That never can enjoy nor wish to have,
What is but meanly in its self a Crime,

But 'tis a Plague, and reigns through all the World.
Faults done by us are like licentious Laws,
Ador'd by all the Rabble, and are easier,
And sooner far obey'd, than what are honest;
And Comets are less dreadful than our Failings———
Where hast thou been?
I thought, dear *Nottingham*, I'd been alone.
   Not. Pardon this bold Intrusion, but my Duty
Urges me farther——— On my Knees I first
Beg Pardon that I am so bold to ask it,
Then, that you wou'd disclose what 'tis afflicts you;
Something hangs heavy on your Royal Mind,
Or else I fear you are not well.
   Queen. Rise, prithee ———
I am in Health, and thank thee for thy Love,
Only a little troubl'd at my People.
I have Reign'd long, and they're grown weary of me;
New Crowns are like new Garlands, fresh and lovely;
My Royal Sun declines toward its West,
They're hot, and tyr'd beneath its Autumn Beams———
Tell me, what says the World of *Essex* coming?
   Not. Much they do blame him for't, but think him brave.
   Queen. What, when the Traytor serv'd me thus!
   Not. Indeed, it was not well.
   Queen. Not well, and was that all?
   Not. It was a very bold and hainous fault.
   Queen. I, was it not? and such a Base Contempt
As he deserves to die for; less than that
Has cost a hundred nearer Favourites Heads,
Since the first Saxon King that Reign'd in *England*
And lately in my Royal Father's time,
Was not brave *Buckingham* for less Condemn'd,
And lost not *Wolsey* all his Church Revenues,
Nay, and his Life too, but that he was a Coward,
And durst not live to feel the stroak of Justice?
Thou know'st it too, and this most vile of Men,
That brave *Northumberland*, and *Westmerland*,
For lesser crimes than his were both beheaded.
   Not. Most true——— Can *Essex* then be thought so guilty
And not deserve to die?
   Queen. To die! to Wrack,
And as his Treasons are the worst of all Mens,
So I will have him plagu'd above the rest,
His Limbs cut off, and plac'd to th' highest View,
Not on low Bridges, Gates, and Walls of Towns,
But on vast Piniacles that touch the Sky
Where all that pass may in derision say,

E

Lo, there is *Effex*, proud ingrateful *Effex*!
Effex that brav'd the Juftice of his Queen——
Is not that well? Why doft not fpeak?
And help the Queen to rail againft this Man.
   Not. Since you will give me leave, I will be plain,
And tell your Majefty what all the World
Says of that proud ingrateful Man;
   Queen. Do fo. Prethee what fays the World of him and me?
   Not. Of you they Speak no worfe than of dead Saints,
And worfhip you no lefs than as their God,
Than Peace, than Wealth, or their Eternal hopes;
Yet do they often wifh with kindeft Tears,
Sprung from the pureft Love, that you'd be pleas'd
To heal their Grievances on *Effex* Charg'd,
And not protect the Traytor by your Power,
But give him up to Juftice and to Shame
For a Revenge of all your Wrongs, and theirs.
   Queen. What, would they then prefcribe me Rules to Govern!
   Not. No more but with Submiffion as to Heaven;
But upon *Effex* they unload Reproaches,
And give him this bad Character,
They fay he is a Perfon (bating his Treafons)
That in his Nobleft, beft Array of Parts,
He fcarcely has enough to make him pafs
For a brave Man, nor yet a Hypocrite,
And that he wears his Greatnefs and his Honours
Foolifh and Proud as Lacquies wear gay Liveries:
Valiant they will admit he is, but then
Like Beafts precipitately Rafh and Bruitifh,
Which is no more commendable in him
Than in a Bear, a Leopard, or a Wolf.
He never yet had Courage over Fortune,
And which to fhew his natural Pride the more,
He roars and ftaggers under fmall Affronts,
And can no more endure the pain than Hell;
Then he's as Covetous, and more Ambitious
Than that firft Fiend that fow'd the Vice in Heav'n,
And therefore was Dethron'd and Tumbl'd thence;
And fo they wifh that *Effex* too may fall.
   Queen. Enough, th'aft rail'd thy felf quite out of Breath;
I'll hear no more —— Blifters upon her Tongue.   [*Afide.*
'Tis bafenefs tho' in thee but to repeat,
What the rude World malicioufly has faid;
Nor dare the vileft of the Rabble think,
Much lefs prophanely fpeak fuch horrid Treafons——
Yet 'tis not what they fay, but what you'd have 'em.
   Not. Did not your Majefty Command me fpeak?

Queen. I did, but then I faw thee on a fudden,
Settle thy Senfes all in eager Poftures,
Thy Lips, thy Speech, and Hands were all prepar'd,
A joyful Red painted thy envious Cheeks,
Malicious Flames flafht in a moment from
Thy Eyes like Lightning from thy o'er-charg'd Soul,
And fir'd thy Breaft, which like a hard ramm'd Piece,
Difcharg'd unmannerly upon my Face.

Not. Pardon, bright Queen, moft Royal and belov'd,
The manner of expreffing of my Duty;
But you your felf began and taught me firft.

Queen. I am his Queen, and therefore may have leave:
May not my felf have Privilege to mould
The thing I made, and ufe it as I pleafe?
Befides he has committed Monftrous Crimes
Againft my Perfon, and has urg'd me far
Beyond the Power of Mortal fuffering.
Me he has wrong'd, but thee he never wrong'd.
What has poor *Effex* done to thee? Thou haft
No Crown that he cou'd hope to gain,
No Laws to break, no Subjects to moleft,
Nor Throne that he cou'd be Ambitious of——
What Pleafure cou'dft thou take to fee
A drowning Man knock'd on the head, and yet
Not wifh to fave the miferable Wretch!

Not. I was to blame.

Queen. No more—— ——
Thou feeft the Queen, the World, and Deftiny
It felf againft this one bad Man, and him
Thou Canft not pity nor excufe.

Not. Madam——

Queen. Be gone, I do forgive thee; and bid *Rutland*   [*Exit* Not-
Come to me ftraight——ha! what have I difclos'd?   tingham.
Why have I chid my Woman for a Fault
Which I wrung from her, and commited firft?
Why ftands my jealous and tormented Soul
A Spy to liften and divulge the Treafons
Spoke again *Effex?*———O you mighty Powers!
Protectors of the Fame of *England*'s Queen,
Let me not know it for a thoufand Worlds,
'Tis dangerous——— But yet it will difcover,
And I feel fomething whifpering to my Reafon,
That fays it is——— O blotted be the Name
For ever from my Thoughts. If it be fo,
And I am ftung with thy Almighty Dart,
I'll die, but I will tear thee from my Heart,
Shake off this hideous Vapour from my Soul,

This

This haughty Earl, the Prince of my Controul;
Banish this Traytor to his Queen's repose,
And blast him with the Malice of his Foes:
Were there no other way his Guilt to prove,
'Tis Treason to infect the Throne with Love.

                          Enter Countess of Essex.

How now my *Rutland*? I did send for you———
I have observ'd you have been sad of late.
Why wearest thou black so long? and why that Cloud,
That mourning Cloud about thy lovely Eyes?
Come, I will find a noble Husband for thee.

    C. *Ess.* Ah! mighty Princess, most ador'd of Queens!
Your Royal Goodness ought to blush, when it
Descends to care for such a Wretch as I am.

    Queen. Why say'st thou so? I love thee well, indeed
I do, and thou shalt find by this 'tis truth———
Injurious *Nottingham*, and I had some
Dispute, and 'twas about my Lord of *Essex*———

    C. *Ess.* Ha!   [*Aside.*

    Queen. So much that she displeas'd me strangely,
And I did send her from my sight in anger.

    C. *Ess.* O that dear name o' th' sudden how it starts me!
Makes every Vein within me leave it's Channel,
To run, and to protect my feeble Heart;
And now my Blood as soon retreats again
To croud with blushes full my guilty Cheeks———
Alas I fear.

    Aside

    Queen. Thou blushest at my Story!

    C. *Ess.* Not I, my Gracious Mistress, but my Eyes
And Cheeks, fir'd and amaz'd with joy, turn'd red
At such a Grace that you were pleas'd to shew me.

    Queen. I'll tell thee then, and ask thee thy advice:
There is no doubt, dear *Rutland*, but thou hear'st
The daily Clamours that my People vent
Against the most unhappy Earl of *Essex*,
The Treasons that they would impeach him of,
And which is worse, this day he is arriv'd
Against my strict Commands, and left Affairs
In *Ireland* desp'rate, headless, and undone.

    C. *Ess.* Might I presume to tell my humble mind,
Such Clamours very often are design'd
More by the Peoples Hate than any Crimes.
In those they wou'd accuse.

    Queen. Thou speak'st my sence;
But oh! dear *Rutland*, he has been to blame———
Lend me thy Breast to lean upon.— O 'tis
A heavy Yoke they wou'd impose on me.

Their Queen, and I am weary of the Load,
And want a Friend like thee to lull my Sorrows.

   C. Eff. Behold thefe tears fprung from fierce Pain and Joy
To fee your wond'rous Grief, your wondrous Pity.
O that kind Heav'n wou'd but inftruct my thoughts,
And teach my Tongue fuch foftning, healing Words,
That it might Charm your Soul, and Cure your Breaft
For ever.

   Queen. Thou art my better Angel then,
And fent to give me everlafting quiet————
Say, Is't not pity that fo brave a Man,
And one that once was reckon'd as a God,
That he fhould be the Author of fuch Treafons?
That he, that was like *Cæfar,* and fo grear,
Has had the Power to make and unmake Kings,
Shou'd ftoop to gain a petty Throne from me?

   C. Eff. I can't believe 'tis in his Soul to think,
Much lefs to act a Treafon againft you,
Your Majefty, whom I have heard him fo
Commend, that Angels words did never flow
With fo much Eloquence, fo rare, fo fweet,
That nothing but the Subject cou'd deferve.

   Queen. Haft thou then heard him talk of me?

   C. Eff. I have,
And as of fo much Excellence, as if
He meant to make a rare Encomium on
The World, the Stars, or what is brighter, Heav'n.
She is, faid he, the Goddefs of her Sex,
So far beyond all Woman-kind befide,
That what in them is moft ador'd, and lov'd,
Their Beauties, Parts, and other Ornaments,
Are but in her the Foils to greater Luftre,
And all Perfections elfe, how rare foever,
Are in her Perfon but as leffer Gleams,
And infinite Beams that ufher ftill the Sun,
But fcarce are vifible amidft her other brightnefs.
And then fhe is fo good, it might be faid,
That whilft fhe lives, a Goddefs reigns in *England:*
For all her Laws are regefter'd in Heaven,
And copy'd thence by her————But then he cry'd,
With a deep figh fetch'd from his loyal Heart,
Well may the World bewail that time at laft,
When fo much Goodnefs fhall on Earth be mortal,
And wretched *England* break its ftubborn Heart.

   Queen. Did he fay all this?

   C. Eff. All this! nay more,
A thoufand times as much, I never faw him

But his discourse was still in praise of you;
Nothing but Raptures fell from *Essex* Tongue:
And all was still the same, and all was you.

　Queen. Such words spoke Loyalty enough.

　C. *Ess.* Then does
Your Majesty believe that he can be
A Traytor?

　Queen. No, yet he has broke the Laws,
And I for shame no longer can protect him;
Nay, durst not see him.

　C. *Ess.* What, not see him, say you!
By that bright Star of Mercy in your Soul,
And listening through your Eyes, let me intreat:
'Tis good, 'tis God-like, and like *England*'s Queen;
Like only her to pity the distress'd————
Will you not grant that he shall see you once?

　Queen. What he
That did defie my absolute Commands,
And brings himself audaciously before me!

　C. *Ess.* Impute it not to that, but to his danger,
That hearing what proceedings here had past
Against his Credit and his Life, he comes
Loyal, tho' unadvised, to clear himself.

　Queen. Well, I will see him then, and see him straight——
Indeed my *Rutland*, I would fain believe
That he is honest still, as he is brave.

　C. *Ess.* O nourish that most kind Belief, 'tis sprung
From Justice in your Royal Soul————Honest!
By your bright Majesty, he's faithful still,
The pure and Virgin Light is less untainted;
The glorious Body of the Sun breeds Gnats,
And Insects that molest its curious Beams;
The Moon has Spots upon her Chrystal Face,
But in his Soul are none————And for his Valour,
The Christian World records its wondrous Story.
Baseness can never mingle with such Courage.
Remember what a Scourge he was to Rebels,
And made your Majesty ador'd in *Spain*
More than their King, that brib'd you with his *Indies*;
And made himself so dreadful to their Fears,
His very Name put Armies to the Rout;
It was enough to say here's *Essex* come;
And Nurses still'd their Children with the Fright.

　Queen. Ha! she's concern'd, Transported!
I'll try her further———— Then he has a Person!

　C. *Ess.* I, in his Person, there you summ up all.
Ah! Loveliest Queen, did you e'er see the like?

The Limbs of *Mars*, and awful Front of *Jove*,
With ſuch a Harmony of Parts as put
To bluſh the Beauties of his Daughter *Venus*,
A Pattern for the God's to make a perfect Man by,
And *Michael Angelo* to frame a Statue
To be ador'd through all the wond'ring World.
 Queen. I can endure no more——Hold *Rutland*,
Thy Eyes are moiſt, thy Senſes in a hurry,
Thy words come crouding one upon another.
Is it a real Paſſion, or extorted?
Is it for *Eſſex* ſake, or for thy Queen's
That makes this furious Tranſport in thy mind?
She loves him——Ah, 'tis ſo——What have I done?
Conjur'd another Storm to Rack my Reſt?
Thus is my Mind with quiet never bleſt,
But like a loaded Bark finds no repoſe,
When 'tis beclam'd, nor when the Weather blows.

Enter Burleigh, *Counteſs of* Nottingham, Rawleigh, *Lords, Attendants.
and Guards.*

 Burl. May't pleaſe your Majeſty the Earl of *Eſſex*
Return'd by your Command, intreats to kneel,
Before you.
 Queen. Now hold out my Treacherous Heart,
Guard well the Breach that this proud Man has made—— } *Aſide.*
Rutland, we muſt defer this Subject till
Some other time——Come hither *Nottingham.*

Enter the Earls of Eſſex *and* Southampton *Attended.*

 Eſſ. Behold your *Eſſex* kneels to clear himſelf
Before his Queen, and now receive his Doom.
 Queen. I muſt divert my Fears——I ſee he takes the way
To bend the ſturdy temper of my Heart——
Well, my Lord, I ſee you can
Withſtand my Anger, as you lately boaſted
You did your Enemies——Were they ſuch Foes
As bravely did reſiſt, or elſe the ſame
You Parly'd with? It was a mighty Courage.
 Eſſ. Well, well, you cruel Fates! well have you found
The way to ſhock the Baſis of a Temper,
That all your Malice elſe cou'd ne'er invent,
And you my Queen to break your Souldier's Heart.
Thunder and Earthquakes, Prodigies on Land
Iv'e born, Devouring Tempeſts on the Seas,
And all the horrid ſtroaks beſide

That.

That Nature e'er invented; yet to me
Your scorn is more———Here take this Traytor,
Since you will have me so; throw me to Dungeons,
Lash me with Iron Rods fast bound in Chains,
And like a Fiend in Darkness let me roar,
It is the nobler Justice of the Two.

    Queen. I see you want no cunning skill to talk,
And daub with words a Guilt you wou'd evade———
But yet, my Lord, if you wou'd have us think
Your Vertues wrong'd, wash off the stain you carry,
And clear your self of Parlying with the Rebels———
Grant Heav'n he does but that, and I am happy.

    Ess. My Parlying with the Enemy?

    Queen. Yes, your secret treating with *Tyrone*, I mean,
And making Articles with *England's* Rebels.

    Ess. Is that alledg'd against me for a Fault,
Put in your Royal Breast by some that are
My false Accusers for a Crime? Just Heav'n!
How easie it is to make a Great Man fall,
'Tis Wise, 'tis Turkish Policy in Courts.
For Treating!
Am I not yet your General, and was
I not so there by virtue of this Staff?
I thought your Majesty had giv'n me Power,
And my Commission had been absolute,
To Treat, to Fight, give Pardons, or Disband:
So much and vast was my Authority,
That you were pleas'd to say as Mirth to others,
I was the first of *English* Kings that Reign'd
In *Ireland.*

    Queen O how soon wou'd I believe,
How willingly approve of such Excuses,
His Answers which to all the Croud are weak———
That large Commission had in it no Power,
That gave you leave to treat with Rebels,
Such as *Tyrone*, and wanted not Authority
To Fight 'em on the least Advantage.

    Ess. The Reason why
I led not forth the Army to the North,
And fought not with *Tyrone*, was, that my Men
Were half consum'd with Fluxes and Diseases,
And those that liv'd, so weakned and unfit,
That they cou'd scarce defend them from the Vultures
That took them for the Carrion of an Army.

    Queen. Oh I can hold no longer, he'll not hide his Guilt
I fear he will undo himself and me———
Name that no more for shame of Thee the Cause,

Nor hide thy Guilt by broaching of a worſe ;
Fain I wou'd tell, but whiſper it in thy Ear,
That none beſides may hear, nay not my ſelf :
How Vitious thou haſt been————Say was not *Eſſex*
The Plague that firſt infected my poor Soldiers,
And kill'd 'em with Diſeaſes ? Was't not he
That loiter'd all the year without one Action,
Whilſt all the Rebels in the North grew bold,
And rally'd daily to the Queen's diſhonour ;
Mean while thou ſtood'ſt and ſaw thy Army rot
In Fenny and unwholſome Camps————Thou haſt
No doubt a Juſt Excuſe for coming too,
In ſpite of all the Letters that I ſent
With my Commands to hinder thee————Be ſilent————
If thou makeſt more ſuch Impudent Excuſes,
Thou'lt raiſe an Anger will be fatal to thee.
   Eſſ. Not ſpeak ! Muſt I be tortur'd on the Rack,
And not be ſuffer'd to diſcharge a Groan ?
Speak ! Yes I will, were there a thouſand Deaths
Stood ready to devour me ; 'tis too plain
My Life's conſpir'd, my Glories all betray'd :
That Vulture *Cecil* there with hungry Noſtrils
Waits for my Blood, and *Rawleigh* for my Charge,
Like Birds of Prey that ſeek out Fighting Fields,
And know when Battel's near : Nay, and my Queen
Has paſt her Vote, I fear, to my Deſtruction.
   Queen. Oh I'me undone ! How he deſtroys my Pity !
Cou'd I bear this from any other Man ?
He pulls and tears the Fury from my Heart
With greater grief and pain, than a fork'd Arrow
Is drawn from forth the Boſom where 'twas lodg'd,
Mild words are all in vain, and loſt upon him————
Proud and Ingrateful Wretch, how durſt thou ſay it !
Know Monſter that thou haſt no Friend but me,
And I have no pretence for it but one,
And that's in Contradiction to the World,
That curſes and abhors thee for thy *Crimes.*
Stir me no more with Anger for thy Life,
Take heed how thou doſt ſhake my wrongs too much,
Leſt they fall thick and heavy on thy Head.
Yet thou ſhalt ſee what a raſh Fool thou art————
Know then that I forgive thee from this Moment
All that is paſt, and this unequal'd Boldneſs,
Give thee that Life thou ſaidſt I did conſpire againſt————
But for your Offices————
   Eſſ. I throw 'em at your feet.   [*Lays his G*
Now baniſh him that planted ſtrength about you,

F

Cover'd this Ifland with my fpreading Lawrels,
Whilft your fafe Subjects flept beneath their fhade.
Give 'em to Courtiers, Sycophants and Cowards,
That fell the Land for Pence and Childrens Portions,
Whilft I retreat to *Africk* in fome Defart,
Sleep in a Den, and Herd with valiant Brutes,
And ferve the King of Beafts, there's more Reward,
More Juftice there than in all Chriftian Courts :
The Lion fpar'd the Man that free'd him from
The Toil, but *Englands* Queen abhors her *Effex.*

   South. My Lord――――

   C. *Eff.* Ah, what will be th' Event of this *!*   [*Afide.*

   Queen. Audacious Traytor.

   Eff. Ha *!*

   South. My Lord, My Lord ; recall your Temper.

   Eff. You faid that I was bold, but now who blames
My Rage ? Had I been ruff as Storms and Tempefts,
Rafh as *Cethegus,* mad as *Ajax* was,
Yet this has ram'd more Powder in my Breaft,
And blown a Magazeen of Fury up――――――
A Traytor *!* Yes, for ferving you fo well ;
For making *England* like the *Roman* Empire
In Great *Auguftus*'s time, renown'd in Peace
At home, and War abroad ; Enriching you
With Spoils both of the wealthy Sea and Land,
More than your *Thames* does bring you in an Age,
And fetting up your Fame to fuch a height
That it appears the Column of the World ;
For tumbling down the Proud Rebellious Earls,
Northumberland and *Weftmerland,* which caus'd
The cutting both their Heads off with an Ax
That fav'd the Crown on yours――――This *Effex* did,
And I'le remove the Traytor from your fight.

   Queen. Stay Sir ; take your reward along with you――――[*Offers to go*]
             the Queen comes up to him, and gives
             him a box on the Ear.

   Eff. Ha ! Furies, Death and Hell ! a Blow !
Has *Effex* had a blow !――――Hold, ftop my Arm   [*Lays hand on*
Some God――Who is't has giv'n it me ? the Queen !   *his Sword.*

   South. What do you mean, my Lord ?

   Queen. Unhand the Villain――――
Durft the vile Slave attempt to murder me ?

   Eff. No, Y'are my Queen, that Charms me, but by all
The fubtilty, and Woman in your Sex
I Swear, that had you been a Man you durft not,
Nay, your bold Father *Harry* durft not this
Have done――――Why fay I him ? not all the *Harry's,*

                                Nor

Nor *Alexander*'s self were he alive,
Shou'd boast of such a Deed on *Essex* done
Without Revenge.

Queen. Rail on, despair, and curse thy foolish Breath,
I'le leave thee like thy Hopes at th' hour of Death,
Like the first Slayer wandring with a Mark,
Shunning the Light, and wishing for the Dark,
In Torments worse than Hell, when thou shalt see
Thou hast by this Curst Chance lost Heav'n and me.

             [*Exeunt* Queen, *&c. Manent* Essex *and* Southampton.

South. What have you done, my Lord ? Your haughty Carriage
Has ruin'd both your self and all your Friends———
Follow the Queen, and humbly on your Knees
Implore Her Mercy, and confess your Fault.

Ess. Ha ! And tell her that I'le take a Blow !
Thou wou'dst not wish thy Friend were such a Slave———
By Heav'n my Cheek has set on Fire my Soul,
And the Disgrace sticks closer to my Heart,
Than did the Son of old *Antipater*'s,
Which cost the Life of his proud Master———Stand off,
Beware you lay not hands upon my Ruine,
I have a load would sink a Legion that
Shou'd offer but to save me.

South. My Lord let us retire,
And shun this barbarous Place.

Ess. I, there thou say'st it———
Abhor all Courts, if thou art brave and wise,
For then thou never shalt be sure to rise;
Think not by doing well a Fame to get,
But be a Villain, and thou shalt be Great.
Here Virtue stands by't self, or not at all,
Fools have Foundations, only brave Men fall,
But if ill Fate, and thy own Merits bring
Thee once to be a Favourite to a King,
It is a Curse that follows Loyalty,
Curst in thy Merits, more in thy Degree,
In all the sport of Chance its chiefest Aim,
Mankind's the *Hunt,* a Favourite is the *Game.*

                                      [*Exeunt.*

Finis Actus Tertii.

                                             Actus

Actus Quartus. Scœna prima.

Countess of Nottingham, Rawleigh.

C. *Nott.* SIR, did you ever see so strange a Scene
　　As *Essex* boldness ? Nay, and which is more
　　To be admir'd, the Queen's prodigious patience !
　　　Raw. So strange, that naught but such a Miracl
Had sav'd him from Death upon the Place.
　　C. *Nott.* She's of a nature wondrous in her Sex,
Not hasty to admire the Beauties, Wisdom,
Valour, and Parts in others though extream,
Because there's so much Excellence in her self,
And thinks that all Mankind should be so too ;
But when once entertain'd, none cherishes,
Exalts, or favours Virtue more than she,
Slow to be mov'd, and in her Rage discreet———
But then the Earl's like an ungovern'd Steed,
That yet has all the Shapes and other Beauties
That are commendable, or sought in one :
His Soul with sullen beams shines in it self,
More Jealous of Mens Eyes, than is the Sun
That will not suffer to be look'd into ;
And there's a Mine of Sulphur in his Breast,
Which when 'tis touch'd or heated, straight takes Fir ;
And tears, and blows up all his Virtues with it.
　　Raw. Ambitious minds feed daily upon Passion,
And ne're can be at rest within themselves,
Because they never meet with Slaves enough
To tread upon, Mechannicks to adore 'em,
And Lords and States-men to have Cringes from ;
Like some of those strange Seas thet I've been on,
Whose tides are always Violent and Rough,
Where Winds are seldom blowing to molest 'em.
Sh' had done a Nobler Justice, if instead of
That School-boys punishment a Blow,
Sh' had snatch'd a Holberd from her nearest Guard,
And thrust it to his heart ; for less than that
Did the bold *Macedonian* Monarch Kill
Clytus his Friend, and braver Souldier far.
　　C. *Nott.* But worse had been th' Event of such a Deed,
For if the afflicted King was hardly brought
From *Clytus* Body, she'd have dy'd o're his.

But how proceed the bold Rebellious Lords
In *Effex* Houfe?

Raw. Still they increafe in number.
The Queen has fent four of her Chiefeft Lords,
And fince I hear the Guards are gone. 'Tis faid,
For his Excufe, that *Blunt* that Fiend of Hell,
And Brand of all his Mafter's wicked Councils,
Has fpread abroad this moft abhorr'd of Lyes,
That I and the Lord *Gray* fhould joyn to murder him.

C. Nott. Already then he's hunted to the Toil,
Where let him roar, and lafh himfelf with Fury,
But never, never fhall get out with ftrugling.
O it o'rejoy'd th' Affront within my Soul,
To fee the Man by all the World ador'd,
That like a Comet fhin'd above, and rul'd below,
To fee him on a fudden from our Eyes
Drop like a Star, and Vanifh in the Ground;
To fee him how he bit the curfed Torture
That durft no farther venture than his Lips,
When he pafs'd by the Guards to hear no Noife,
No Room for Mighty *Effex* was proclaim'd;
No Caps, no Knees, nor Welcomes to falute him,
Then how he Chaft, and ftarted like a Deer
With the fierce Dart faft fticking in his fide,
And finds his fpeedy death where e're he runs!

Raw. Behold the Queen and the whole Court appear.

Enter the Queen, Burleigh, *Countefs of* Nottingham, *Lords, Attendants and Guards.*

Queen. Are the Rebellious Earls then apprehended?
Burl. They are, thanks to the Almighty Powers,
And the Eternal Fortune of your Majefty.
Queen. And how did you proceed with my Command:
And how did the Rebels act?
Burl. Moft Audacioufly:
The Four Lords, chiefeft of your Private Council,
Sent thither by your Majefties Commiffion,
Came to the Rebels Houfe, but found the Gates
Guarded and fhut againft them; yet at laft
Telling they brought a Meffage from the Queen,
They were admitted, all befides, but him
That bore the Seal before the Chancellor
Deny'd: Entring, they faw the outward Court
Fill'd with a number of promifcuous Perfons,
The chief of which bold Traytors in the midft
Stood the two Earls of *Effex* and *Southampton,*

Of whom your faithful Meſſengers with loud
And loyal Voices did demand the Cauſe
Of their unjuſt Aſſembly, telling them
All real Grievances ſhou'd be redreſs'd ;
But ſtraight their words were Choak'd by louder Cries,
And by the Earl's Command with Inſolence
The People drove 'em to a ſtrong Apartment
Belonging to the Houſe, ſetting a Guard
Of Muskets at the Door, and threatning them
That they ſhou'd there be kept cloſe Priſoners
Till the next Morning that the Earl return'd
From viſiting his Friends the Citizens.

   Queen. O horrid Inſolence ! Attempt my Council !
My neareſt Friends ! Well, *Eſſex,* well,
I thank thee for the Cure of my Diſeaſe ;
Thou goeſt the readieſt way to give me eaſe——
The City ſay'ſt ! What did he in the City ?

   Burl. There, as I learn't from many that Confeſt,
He was inform'd the Citizens would riſe,
Which to promote, he went diſguis'd like one
Whom evil Fortune had bereav'd of Sence,
And almoſt ſeem'd as pitiful a Wretch
As *Harpagus,* that fled all o're diſmember'd
To fond *Aſtyages,* to gain the Truſt
Of all his *Median* Army to betray it.
His Head was bare, the heat and duſt had made
His Manly Face compaſſionate to behold, which he
So well did uſe, that ſometimes with a voice
That uſher'd Tears both from himſelf and them,
And ſometimes with a popular Rage he ran
With Fury through the Streets. To thoſe that ſtood
Far off he bended and made taking Signs :
To thoſe about him rais'd his Voice aloud,
And humbly did beſeech 'em for a Guard,
Told 'em he was attempted to be murder'd
By ſome the Chief of th' Court, then counted all his Wound
Unſtrip'd his Veſt, and ſhew'd his naked Scars,
Telling them what great Wonders he had done,
And wou'd do more to ſerve 'em and their Children ;
Begging ſtill louder to the ſtinking Rabble,
And ſweated too ſo many eager drops, as if
He had been pleading for *Rome*'s Conſulſhip.

   Queen. How came he taken ?

   Burl. After he had us'd
Such ſubtile means to gain your Subjects Hearts,
(Your Citizens that ever were moſt faithful,
And too well grounded in their Loyalties

To be ſeduc'd from ſuch a Queen ;) and finding
That none began to Arm in his behalf;
Fear and Confuſion of his horrid Guilt
Poſſeſt him, and deſparing of ſucceſs,
Attempted ſtraight to walk through *Ludgate* home;
But being reſiſted by ſome Companies
Of the Train'd Bands that ſtood there in defence,
He ſoon retreated to the neareſt Stairs,
And ſo came back by Water at the Time
When your moſt Valiant Souldiers with their Leader-
Enter'd his houſe, and took *Southampton* and the reſt.
Th' affrighted Earl Defenceleſs both in mind
And Body, without the Power to help himſelf;
And being full of Horror in his Thoughts,
Was forc'd to run for ſhelter in the Room
Of a ſmall Summer-Houſe upon the *Thames,*
Which when the Souldiers came to ſearch, and found him ;
Who then had Eyes and did not melt for Pity !
To ſee the High, the Gallant *Eſſex* there
Trembling and Panting like the frighted Quarry
Whom the fierce Hawk had in his eager Eye.
　Queen. Ha ! by my Stars, I think the mournful Tale
Has almoſt made thee weep——Can *Eſſex* miſeries
Then force Compaſſion from thy flinty Breaſt ?
'A weeps, the Crocodile weeps o're his Prey !
How wretched and how low then art thou faln,
That ev'n thy Barbarous Hunters can neglect
Their Rage, and turn their cruel ſport to pity!
What then muſt be my Lot ? how many ſighs,
How many Griefs, Repentances and Horrors
Muſt I eternally endure for this ?
Where is the Earl ?
　Burl. Under ſufficient Guard,
In order to his ſending to the Tower.
　Queen. Ha, in the Tower ! How durſt they ſend him there
Without my Order ?
　Burl. Th' Earls are yet without
In the Lieutenant's Cuſtody, who waits
But to receive your Majeſties Command
To carry 'em thither.
　Queen. What ſhall I do now ?
Wake me thou watchful Genius of thy Queen,
Rouſe me, and Arm now againſt my Foe,
Pity's my Enemy, and Love's my Foe.
And both have equally conſpir'd with *Eſſex.*
Ha! Shall I then refuſe to puniſh him ?
Condemn the Slave that diſobey'd my Orders,

　　　　　　　　　　　　　Aſide.

　　　　　　　　　　　　　　　That

That brav'd me to my Face, and did attempt
To murder me, then went about to gain
My Subjects Hearts and seize my Crown.   } *Aside.*
Now by my thousand wrongs 'a dies, dies quickly,
And I cou'd stab his Heart, if I but thought
The Traytor in it to corrupt it————————Away
And send him to the Tower with speed————Yet hold.

   C. *Nott.* The Queen's distracted how to save the Earl,——   } *Aside.*
Her Study put my Hatred on the Rack.

   Queen. Who is it thou wou'dst kill with so much hast?
Is it not *Essex*? Him thou didst create,
And Crown'd his Morning with full Rays of Honours?
Whilst he return'd 'em with whole springs of Lawrels,   } *Aside.*
Fought for thy Fame a hundred times in Blood,
And ventur'd twice as many Lives for thee;
And shall I then for one rash act of his
Of which I was the cruel Cause, Condemn him?

   C. *Nott.* Her Rage ebbs out, and Pity flows apace.   [*Aside.*

   Queen. Do what you will, my Stars, do as you please
Just Heav'n, and censure *England*'s Queen for it,
Yet *Essex* I must see, and then who e're thou art
That when I'm dead shall call this tender Fault,
This only action of my Life in Question,
Thou canst at worst but say that it was Love,
Love that does never cease to be obey'd,   } *Aside.*
Love that has all my Power and strength betray'd,
Love that sways wholly like the Cause of things.
Kings may rule Subjects, but Love reigns o're Kings,
Sets bounds to Heav'ns high Wrath when 'tis severe,
And is the greatest Bliss and Virtue there.————
Carry *Southampton* to the Tower Straight,
But *Essex* I will see before he goes————————
Now help me Art, check ev'ry Pulse within me,
And let me feign a Courage tho' I've none————————

Enter Essex *with Guards.*

Behold 'a comes with such a Pomp of misery?
Greatness in all he shews, and nothing makes   } *Aside.*
Him less, but turns to be Majestick in him.
All that are present for a while withdraw,
All leave the Prisoner here with me unguarded.
                [*Exeunt. Manent* Queen *and* Essex.

   Ess. Thus tho' I am Condemn'd and hated by you,
A Traytor by your Royal Will proclaim'd;   [Essex *kneels.*
Thus do I bless my Queen, and all those Powers
Th' have inspir'd her with such tender mercy.

As once to hear her dying *Essex* speak,
And now receive his Sentence from your Lips,
Which let it be my Life or Death, they're both
Alike to me, from you my Royal Mistress :
And thus I will receive my Doom, and wish
My Knees might ever till my dying Minute
Cleave to the Earth, as now they do in token of
The choicest, humblest begging of the Blessing.

  Queen. Pray rise, my Lord. You see that I dare venture
To leave my self without a Guard between us.

  Ess. Fairest that e're was *England's* Queen, you need not——
The time has been that *Essex* has been thought
A Guard, and, being near you, has been more
Than Crouds of Mercinary Slaves ;
And is he not so now ? O think me rather,
Think me a Traytor, if I can be so
Without a thought against your Precious Life,
But wrong me not with that : For by your self,
By your bright self that rules o're all my Wishes,
I swear I would not touch that Life, to be
As Great as you, the greatest Prince on Earth ;
Lightning shou'd blast me first,
E're I wou'd touch the Person of my Queen,
Less gentle than the Breeze.

  Queen. O y'are become a wondrous Penitent,
My Lord, the time has been you were not so :
Then you were haughty, and because you urg'd me,
Urg'd me beyond the suffering of a Saint,
To strike you, which a King wou'd have obey'd ;
Then straight your Malice led you to the City,
Tempting my Loyal Subjects to Rebel,
Laying a Plot how to surprize the Court,
Then seize my Person with my chiefest Council,
To Murder them, and I to beg your Mercy ;
This, this the wond'rous Faithful *Essex* did,
Thou whom I rais'd from the vile Dust of man,
And plac'd thee as a Jewel in my Crown,
And bought thee dearly for my Favour, at the rate
Of all my Peoples Grievances and Curses,
Yet thou didst this, ingrateful Monster, this
And all, for which as surely thou shalt dye,
Dye like the foulest and the worst Ingrate ;
But Fetters now have humbled you, I see.

  Ess. O hear me speak, most injur'd Majesty,
Brightest of Queens, Goddess of Mercy too,
Oh think not that the Fear of Death or Prisons
Can e're disturb a Heart like mine, or make it

More Guilty, or more senfible of Guilt.
All that y'are pleas'd to fay, I now confefs,
Confefs my Mifery, my Crime, my fhame ;
Yet neither Death nor Hell fhou'd make me own it,
But true Remorfe and duty to your felf,
And Love———I dare ftand Candidate with Heav'n,
Who loves you moft and pureft.

   Queen. How he awakes me,
And all my faculties begin to liften,
Steal to my Eyes, and tread foft paces to
My Ears as loath to be difcover'd, yet
As loath to lofe the Syrens Charming Song.
Help me a little now my cautious Angel.———
I muft confefs I formerly believ'd fo,
And I acknowledg'd it by my Rewards.

   Ef. You have, but oh what has my Rafhnefs done !
And what has not my Guilt Condemn'd me to !
Seated I was in Heav'n, where once that Angel,
That haughty Spirit Reign'd that tempted me,
But now thrown down, like him, to worfe then Hell.

   Queen. I, think on that, and like that Fiend roar ftill
In Torments, when thou may'ft have been moft happy———
There I out-did my ftrength, and feel my Rage
Recoil upon me, like a foolifh Child
Who firing of a Gun as much as he can lift,
Is blafted with the fury of the blow.

   Ef. Moft bleft of Queens ! her Doom, her very Anger's kind,
And I will fuffer it as willingly
As your loud wrongs inftruct you to inflict.
I know my Death is nigh, my Enemies
Stand like a Guard of Furies ready by you
To intercept each Sigh, kind Wifh, or Pity,
E're it can reach to Heav'n in my Defence,
And Dafh it with a Cloud of Accufations.

   Queen. Ha! I begin to dread the Danger nigh,
Like an unskilful Swimmer that has waded
Beyond his Depth, I am caught, and almoft drown'd,
In Pity———What ! And no one near to help me !

   Ef. My Father once too truly skill'd in Fate,
In my firft blooming Age to rip'ning Glory,
Bid me beware my Six and Thirtieth year,
That year faid he will fatal to thee prove,
Something like Death, or worfe than Death will feize thee.
Too well I find that cruel time's at hand,
For what can e're more fatal to me prove
Than my loft Fame, and lofing of my Queen !

   Queen.

Afide.

Afide.

Afide.

Queen. 'Tis fo, 'tis true, nor is it in my Power
To help him——Ha! Why is it not! What hinders!
Who dares, or thinks to contradict my Will!
Is it my Subjects or my Vertue ftays me?
No, Virtue's patient and abhors Revenge,
Nay, fometimes weeps at Juftice——'Tis not Love——
Ah call it any thing but that; 'tis Mercy,
Mercy that pities Foes when in diftrefs,
Mercy the Heav'ns Delights——
My Lord I fear your hot-fpur Violence
Has brought you to the very brink of Fate,
And 'tis not in my Power if I'd the will,
To fave you from the Sentence of the Law.
The Lords that are to be your equal Judges,
The Houfe has chofe already, and to morrow,
So foon your Tryal is to be. The People
Cry loud for Juftice; therefore I'le no more
Repeat my Wrongs, but think you are the man
That once was Loyal.
   Eff. Once!——
   Queen. Hold!——For that Reafon I will not upbraid you,
To Triumph o're a miferable man
Is bafe in any, in a Queen far worfe——
Speak now, my Lord, and think what's in my Power
That may not wrong your Qneen, and I will grant you——
So——I am fure in this I have not err'd.
   Eff. Bleft be my Queen, in Mercy rich as Heav'n——
Now, now my Chains are light——Come welcome Death,
Come all you Spirits of Immortality,
And waft my Soul unto his bright abode,
That gives my Queen this goodnefs: Let me then
Moft humbly and devoutly ask two things,
The Firft is, if I am Condemn'd,
That Execution may be done within
The Tower Walls, and fo I may not fuffer
Upon a publick Scaffold to the World.
   Queen. I grant it——O, and wifh I cou'd do more.
   Eff. Eternal Bleffings Crown your Royal Head,
The next, the extreameft Blifs my Soul can covet
And carry with it to the other World,
As a firm Pafport to the Powers incens'd,
Say you have pardon'd me, and have forgot
The Rage, the Guilt, and Folly of your *Effex.*
   Queen. Ha! What fhall I do now?
Look to thy felf, and Guard thy Character——
Go cure your Fame, and make your felf but what I wifh you,
Then you fhall find that I am ftill your Queen——

Afide.

[*Afide.*

[*Afide.*

}*Afide.*

But

But that you may not see I'm Covetous
Of my Forgiveness, take it from my Heart;
I freely pardon now what e're y'ave done
Amiss to me, and hope you will be quitted;
Nay, I not only hope it, but shall pray for it,
My Prayers to Heav'n shall be that you may clear
Your self.

Ess. O most Renown'd and God-like Mercy!
O let me go, your goodness is too bright
For sinful Eyes like mine, or like the Fiend
Of Hell, when dasht from the Ætherial Light,
I shall shoot downwards with my weight of Curses,
Cleave and be chain'd for ever to the Center. ———

Queen. He is going, I, but whither? To his Tryal,
To be Condemn'd perhaps, and then to dye;
If so, what Mercy hast thou shew'd in that!
Pity and Pardon! Poor Amends for Life!
If those be well, a Crocodile is blameless
That weeps for Pity, yet devours his Prey,
And dare not I do more for *Essex*, I
That am a Woman, and in Woman-kind
Pity's their Nature, therefore I'm resolv'd
It shall be in's own Power to save his Life.
If I shall sin in this, Witness just Heav'n
'Tis mercy like your selves that draws me to't,
And you'l forgive me, tho' the World may not.———
My Lord, perhaps we ne're may meet again,
And you in Person may not have the Power
T'implore what I do freely grant you, therefore
That you may see you have not barely forc'd
An empty Pity from me, here's a Pledge,
I give it from my Finger with this promise,
That whensoever you return this Ring,   *[Gives him a Ring.*
To grant in lieu of it what e're you ask.

Ess. Thus I receive it with far greater Joy   *[Receives it on his knees.*
Than the poor Remnant of Mankind that saw
The Rain-bow Token in the Heav'ns, when straight
The Floods abated, and the Hills appear'd,
And a new smiling World the Waves brought forth.

Queen. No more, be gone, fly with thy safety hence,
Left horrid, dread repentance seize my Soul,
And I recall this strange misdeed———Here take   *[Enter the rest with*
Your Prisoner, there he is, to be condemn'd   *the Guards]*
Or quitted by the Law———Away with him!   *[Exeunt Guard with*
Now, *Nottingham,* thy Queen is now at rest,   *the Earl.]*
And *Essex* Fate is now my least of Troubles.

Enter

Aside. (bracketed passage)

Enter Countess of Essex *running and weeping, then kneels before the Queen and holds her by her Robe.*

C. Eff. Where is my Queen? Where is my Royal Miſtreſs?——
I throw my ſelf for mercy here.

Queen. What mean'ſt thou?

C. Eff. Here I will kneel, here with my humble Body
Faſt rooted to the Earth, as I am to ſorrow,
No moiſture but my Tears to nouriſh me,
Nor Air but ſighs, till I ſhall grow at laſt
Like a poor ſhrivell'd Trunk blaſted with Age
And Grief, and never think to riſe again
Till I've obtain'd the Mercy I implore.

Queen. Thou doſt amaze me.

C. Eff. Here let me grow the abjeĉt'ſt thing on Earth,
A deſpis'd Plant beneath the mighty Cedar;
Yet if you will not pity me, I ſwear
Theſe Arms ſhall never ceaſe, but graſping ſtill
Your Royal Robe, ſhall hold you thus for ever.

Queen. Prythee be quick, and tell me what thou'dſt have.

C. Eff. I dare not, yet I muſt——My Silence will
Be Death, my Puniſhment can be no more.
Prepare to hear, but learn to pity firſt,
For 'tis a Story that will ſtart your Patience.——
O ſave the Earl of *Eſſex,* ſave his Life,
My Lord whom you've condemn'd to Priſons ſtraight,
And ſave my Life, who am no longer *Rutland,*
But *Eſſex* faithful Wife——he is my Husband.

Queen. Thy Husband!

C. Eff. Yes, too true it is I fear,
By th'awful darting Fury in your Eyes,
The threatning Prologue of our utter Ruines.
Marri'd we were in ſecret e're my Lord
Was ſent by you t'his fatal Government
In *Ireland.*

Queen. Then thou art wedded to thy Grave——
Doſt think by this, in multiplying Treaſons,
And boldly braving me with them before
My Face, to ſave thy wicked Husband's Life?
What will my reſtleſs Fate do with me now!
Why doſt thou hold me ſo? take off thy hands.   [*Aſide.*

C. Eff. Alas, I ask not mine; if that will pleaſe you
I'll glut you with my Torments; aĉt what e're
Your Fury can invent; but 'tis for him,
My Lord, my Love, the Soul of my deſires.
My Love's not like the common Rate of womens,

It

It is a *Phœnix*, there's not one such more :
How gladly would I burn like that rare Bird,
So that the Ashes of my heart cou'd purchase
Poor *Essex* Life and Favour of my Princess.

   Queen. Wou'd I were loose 'mong Wilds, or any where
In any Hell but this——Why say I Hell ?   } *Aside.*
Can there be melting Lead, or Sulphur yet
To add more Pain to what my Breast indures ?
Why dost thou hang on me, and tempt me still ?

   C. Ess. O throw me not away——Wou'd you but please
To feel my throbbing Breast, you might perceive,
At ev'ry name, and very thought of *Essex*,
How my Blood starts, and Pulses beat for fear,
And shake and tear my Body like an Earth-quake,
And ah, which cannot chose but stir your Heart
The more to pity me, th' unhappy frighted Infant,
The tender Off-spring of our guilty Joys,
Pleads for it's Father in the Womb,
As now its wretched Mother does.

   Queen. Quickly
Unloose her Hands, and take her from my sight.

   C. Ess. O you will not——you'l hear me first, and grant me,
Grant me poor *Essex* Life——Shall *Essex* live ?
Say, but you'l pardon him before I go ?

   Queen. Help me——Will no one ease me of this Burthen ?

   C. Ess. Oh I'm too weak for these inhumane Creatures,   [*The Women*
My Strength's decay'd, my Joynts and Fingers num'd,   *take off her*
And can no longer hold, but fall I must.   *hold.*
Thus like a miserable Wretch that thinks
H'as 'scap'd from drowning, holding on a Rock
With fear and Pain, and his own weight opprest,
And dasht by ev'ry Wave that shrinks his hold,   [*She falls down with*
At length lets go, and drops into the Sea,   *faintness.*]
And cryes for help, but all in vain like me.

   Queen. Be gone, and be deliver'd of thy shame.
Let the vile Insect live, and grow to be
A Monster baser, hotter, worser far
Than the ingrateful Parents that begot it.

   C. Ess. Ah cruel most remorseless Princess hold,
What has it done to draw such Curses from you !

   Queen. Go, let her be close Prisoner in her Chamber.

   C. Ess. Since I must go, and from my *Essex* part,
Despair and Death at once come seize my Heart ;
Shut me from Light, from Day ne're to be seen,
By humane kind, nor my more cruel Queen ;
Yet bless her Heav'n, and hear my Loyal Prayer,
May you ne're Love like me, nor ne're despair,

Ne're

Ne're see the Man at his departing Breath
Whom you so love, and fain wou'd save from Death ;
Least Heav'n be deaf as you are to my Cry,
And you run mad, and be as curst as I.

[*Exit C. Essex, carried away by Women.*

Queen. She's gone, but at her parting shot a truth
Into my Breast, has pierc'd my Soul,———
Why was I Queen ? And why was I not *Rutland* ?
Then had my Princess, as my self did now,
Giv'n *Essex* such a Ring, and the Reward
Had then been mine, as now the Torment is———
O wretched State of Monarchs ! theirs is still
The Business of the World, and all the Pains,
Whilst happy Subjects sleeps beneath their Gains ;
The meanest Hind rules in his humble House,
And nothing but the Day sees what he does,
But Princes, like the Queen of Night so high,
Their Spots are seen by every Vulgar Eye ;
And as the Sun, the Planets glorious King,
Gives Life and Growth to every Mortal thing,
And by his Motion all the World is blest,
Whilst he himself can never be at Rest ;
So if there are such Blessings in a Throne,
Kings raign 'em down, while they themselves have none.

[*Exeunt Omnes.*

Finis Actus Quart.

Actus Quintus. Scæna prima.

Sir Walter Rawleigh *with the Queens Guards,
The Lieutenant of the Tower.*

Raw. MR. *Lieutenant*, here expires my Charge ;
I received Orders from her Majesty,
And the Lord Steward, to return the Prisoners
Safe in your Custody, and with you I leave 'em,
With charge to have 'em in a readiness,
For Execution will be very speedy.

Lieut. I shall, Sir.

Enter the Countess of Nottingham.

Raw. Ha ! The Lady *Nottingham* !
What makes her here ?

Nott.

Nott. Where is my Lord of *Essex* ?
I am commanded straight to speak with him,
And bring a Message from her Majesty.
  Raw. Madam,
What News can this strange Visit bring ?
How fares the Queen ? Are her Resolves yet stedfast ?
  Nott. No, when she heard that *Essex* was condemn'd,
She started and look'd pale, then blushing red,
And said that Execution should be straight,
Then stopt, and said she'd hear first from the Earl :
So she retir'd and past an hour in Thought,
None daring t'interrupt her, till in haste
She sent for me, Commanding me to go
And tell my Lord from her, she cou'd resist,
No longer her Subjects loud demands for Justice,
And therefore wisht, if he had any Reasons
That were of weight to stay his Execution,
That he wou'd send 'em straight by me ; then blush'd
Again, and sigh'd, and prest my hand,
And pray'd me to be secret, and deliver
What *Essex* shou'd return in answer to her.
  Raw. I know not what she means, but doubt th'Event; ———
You can tell best the cause of her disturbance.
I will to *Burleigh*, and then both of us
Will make Attempts to recollect the Queen.
                         [*Exit* Rawleigh *and Guards.*

  Nott. Pray bring me to my Lord.
  Lieut. Madam, I will acquaint him that y'are here.   [*Exit Lieut.*
  Nott. Now Dragons Blood distill through all my Veins,
And Gaul instead of Milk swell up my breasts,
That nothing of the Woman may appear,
But horrid Cruelty, and fierce Revenge———

                    Enter Essex.

He comes with such a Gallantry and Port,
As if his Miseries were Harbingers,
And Death the State to set his Person out———
Wrongs less than mine, though in a Tiger's Breast,
Might now be reconcil'd to such an Object ;
But slighted Love my Sex can ne're forget.
  Ess. Madam, this is a Miracle of Favour,
A double goodness in my Royal Mistress,
T'imploy the fair, the injur'd *Nottingham*,
And 'tis no less in you to condescend
To see a wretch like me that has deserv'd
No favour at your hands.

                                                      A

Nott. No more, my Lord, the Queen,
The gracious Queen commends her Pity to you,
Pity by me that owe a great deal more
You know, and wish that I were once your Queen,
To give you what my heart has had so long in store.

Eff. Then has my Death more Charms than Life can promise,
Since my Queen pities me, and you forgive me.

Nott. Hold, good my Lord, that is not all, she sends
To know if you can any thing propose
To mitigate your Doom, and stay your Death,
Which else can be no longer than this Day.
Next, if y'are satisfy'd with ev'ry passage
In your late Tryal, if 'twere fair and legal,
And if y'ave those Exceptions that are real
She'll answer them ?

Eff. Still is my Death more welcom,
And Life wou'd be a burthen to my Soul,
Since I can ne're requite such Royal Goodness.
Tell her then, fair and charitable Messenger,
That *Essex* does acknowledge every Crime,
His Guilt unworthy of such wond'rous Mercy,
Thanks her bright Justice, and the Lords his Judges,
For all was Gracious and Divine like her ;
And I have now no Injustice to accuse,
Nor Enemy to blame that was the Cause,
Nor Innocence to save me but the Queen.

Nott. Ha, is this true ! How he undoes my Hopes *!*   [*Aside.*
And is that all ? have you not one Request
To ask, that you can think the Queen will grant you ?

Eff. I have, and humbly 'tis that she wou'd please
To spare my Life ; not that I fear to dye,
But in submission to her Heav'nly Justice,
I own my Life a forfeit to her Power,
And therefore ought to beg it of her Mercy.

Nott: If this be real, my Revenge is lost.   [*Aside.*
Is there naught else that you rely upon,
Only submitting to the Queen's meer Mercy,
And barely asking her so great a Grace ?
Have you no other hopes ?

Eff. Some Hopes I have.

Nott. What are they, pray, my Lord ? declare 'em boldly,
For to that only purpose I am sent.

Eff. Then I am happy, happiest of mankind,
Blest in the rarest mercy of my Queen,
And such a Friend as you, blest in you both ;
The Extasie will let me hold no longer——
Behold this Ring the Purport of my Life ;

At laſt y'ave pull'd the ſecret from my Heart.
This precious token——
Amidſt my former Triumphs in her favour
She took from off her Finger, and beſtow'd
On me——Mark, with the Promiſe of a Queen,
Of her bright ſelf leſs failing than an Oracle,
That in what Exigence or State ſo e're
My Life was in, that time when I gave back,
Or ſhou'd return this Ring again to her,
She'd then deny me nothing I cou'd ask.

   Nott. O give it me, my Lord, and quickly let
Me bear it to the Queen, and ask your Life.

   Eſſ. Hold, generous Madam, I receiv'd it on   [*Kneels and*
My Knees, and on my Knees I will reſtore it.   *gives* Not-
Here take it, but conſider what you take: tingham *the*
'Tis the Life, Blood, and very Soul of *Eſſex.*   *Ring.*
I've heard that by a skilful Artiſt's Hand,
The Bowels of a wretch were taken out,
And yet he liv'd ; you are that gallant Artiſt,
O touch it as you would the Seals of Life,
And give it to my Royal Miſtreſs Hand,
As you wou'd pour my Blood back in its empty Channels,
That gape and thirſt like Fiſhes on the Ouſe
When Streams run dry, and their own Element
Forſakes 'em ; if this ſhou'd in the leaſt miſcarry,
My Life's the purchaſe that the Queen will have for't.

   Nott. Doubt you my care, my Lord ? I hope you do not.

   Eſſ. I will no more ſuſpect my Fate, nor you:
Such Beauty, and ſuch Merits muſt prevail.

Enter a Gentleman.

   Gent. The Earl of *Southampton* having leave,
Deſires to ſpeak with you, my Lord.

   Nott. Repoſe
Your mind, and take no thought but to be happy ;
I'll ſend you Tidings of a laſting Life.

   Eſſ. A longer and much happier Life attend
Both my good Queen and you.   [*Exit* Eſſex.

   Nott. Farewell, my Lord——
Yes, a much longer Life than thine, I hope,
And if thou chance to dream of ſuch ſtrange things,
Let it be there where lying Poets feign
Elyſium is, where Myrtles lovely ſpread,
Trees of delicious Fruit invite the Taſte,
And ſweet *Arabian* Plants delight the Smell,
'Where pleaſant Gardens dreſt with curious care

By Lovers Ghosts, shall recreate thy Fancy,
And there perhaps thou soon shalt meet again
With amorous *Rutland,* for she cannot choose
But be Romantick now, and follow thee———

Enter a Gentlewoman.

Wom. Madam, the Queen.
Nott. Ha! that's unlucky———She come to the Tower!
Yet 'tis no matter; see him I am sure
She will not, or at worst will be perswaded.

Enter the Queen.

Queen. How now, dear *Nottingham,* hast seen the Earl?
I left *White-hall,* because I cou'd not rest
For Crowds that hollow'd for their Executions,
And others that Petition'd for the Traytors.
Quick, tell me, hast thou done as I Commanded?
Nott. Yes, Madam, I have seen and spoke with him.
Queen. And what has he said to thee for himself?
Nott. At my first converse with him I did find him
Not totally despairing, nor complaining;
But yet a haughty Melancholy
Appear'd in all his Looks, that shew'd him rather
Like one that had more Care
Of future Life than this.
Queen. Well, but what said he,
When thou awaked'st him with hopes of Pity?
Nott. To my first Question put by your Command,
Which was to know if he were satisfied
In the proceedings of his lawful Tryal,
He answer'd with a careless Tone and Gesture,
That it was true, and he must needs confess
His Trial lookt most fair to all the World;
But yet he too well knew,
The Law that made his Actions Treason,
Consulted but with Foes and Circumstances,
And never took from Heav'n or *Essex* Thoughts
A President or Cause that might condemn him,
For if they had the least been read in either,
They wou'd have quickly found his Innocence.
Queen. Ha!
Nott. That was but the Prologue, mark what follows.
Queen. What, durst he be so bold to brand my Justice!
Nott. I pray'd that he wou'd urge that Sence no more,
But since he was condemn'd and stood in need

H 2

Of Mercy, to implore it of your Majefty,
And beg his Life which you would not deny :
For to that end I faid that you were pleas'd
To fend me to him, and then told him all,
Nay more than you commanded me to fay.

   Queen. What faid he then ? that alter'd him I hope.

   Nott. No, not at all, but as I have feen a Lyon
That has been play'd withall with gentle ftroaks,
Has at the laft been jefted into Madnefs ;
Soon on a fudden ftarted into Paffion
The furious Earl, his Eyes grew fiery red,
His words precipitate, and fpeech diforder'd ;
Let the Queen have my blood, faid he, 'tis that
She longs for, pour it to my Foes to drink
As Hunters when the Quarry is run down,
Throw to the Hounds his Intrails for Reward.
I have enough to fpare, but by the Heav'ns
I fwear, were all my Veins like Rivers full,
And if my Body held a Sea of Blood,
I'de lofe it all to the laft Innocent drop,
Before I'de like a Villain beg my Life.

   Queen. Hold, *Nottingham,* and fay th'art not in earneft——
Can this be true, fo impudent a Traytor *!*

   Nott. That's but the Glofs, the Colour of his Treafon,
But after he did paint himfelf to th' Life.
Wou'd the Queen, faid he, have me own a Treafon,
Impofe upon my felf a Crime, the Law
Has found me guilty of by her Command;
And fo by asking of my Forfeit Life,
Clear and proclaim her Juftice to the World,
And ftain my felf for ever ; no I'll dye firft.

   Queen. Enough, I'll hear no more, you wrong him, 'tis
Impoffible he fhou'd be fuch a Devil.

   Nott. Madam I've done.

   Queen. I prithee pardon me——
But could he fay all this *!*

   Nott. He did, and more ;
But 'tis no matter, 'twill not be believ'd
If I fhould tell the half of what he utter'd,
How Infolent and how Profane he us'd you.

   Queen. You need not, I had rather
Believe it all than put you to the trouble
To tell it o're again, and me to hear it.
Then I am loft, betray'd by this falfe Man.
My Courage, Power, my Pity all betray'd,
And like that Gyant, Patriarch of the *Jews,*
Bereft at once both of his fight and ftrength

By Treacherous Foes, I wander in the dark,
By *Effex* weakened, and by *Effex* blinded;
But then as he pray'd that his ftrength might grow,
At once to be reveng'd on them and dye,
So grant me Heav'n but fo much Refolution
To grope my way where I may lay but hold
On whatfoe're this huge *Coloffus* ftands,
I'll pull the Scaffold down, down, tho o're my Head,
And lofe my Life to be reveng'd on his——

Afide.

Well *Nottingham*, I have but one word more,
Talkt not this wicked Creature of no Reafon,
No Obligation that I had to fave
His Life ?

Nott. No, but far worfe than I have told you.
Queen. Sure thou art moft unhappy in ill News!
No Promife, nor Token did he fpeak of?

Nott. Not the leaft word, and if there are fuch things,
I do fuppofe he keeps 'em to himfelf,
For reafons that I know not.

Queen. 'Tis moft falfe,
He needs muft tell thee all, and thou betray'ft him.

Nott. Your Majefty does me wrong——
Queen. Hear me——
Oh I can hold no longer——Say, fent he
No Ring, no Token, nor no Meffage by thee?

Nott. Not any on the forfeit of my Life.
Queen. Thou lyeft——Can Earth Produce fo vile a Creature!——
Hence from my fight, and fee my Face no more——
Yet tarry *Nottingham*——Come back again.
This may be true, and I am ftill the Wretch

[*Afide.*

To blame and to be pity'd——Prithee pardon me;
Forget my Rage, thy Queen is forry for't.

Nott. I wou'd your Majefty inftead of me,
Had fent a Perfon that you cou'd confide in,
Or elfe that you wou'd fee the Earl your felf.

Queen. Prithee no more; go to him!
No, but I'll fend a Meffage for his Head.
His Head's the Token that my wrongs require.
And his bafe Blood the Stream to quench my Fury.——
Prithee invent: for thou art wondrous witty
At fuch inventions; teach my feeble Malice
How to torment him with a thoufand Deaths,
Or what is worfe than Death——Speak, my *Medea*,
And thou wilt then oblige thy Queen for ever.

Nott. Firft Sign an Order for his Execution.
Queen. Say, it is done, but how to torture him!

Nott

Nott. Then as the Lords are carrying to the Block,
Condoling both their fad Misfortunes,
Which to departing Souls is fome delight,
Order a Pardon for *Southampton's* Life,
It will be worfe than Hell to *Effex* Soul
Where 'tis a going, to fee his Friend fnatcht from him,
And make him curfe his fo much Pride and Folly
That loft his own Life, in exchange for his.
   Queen. That was well thought on !
   Nott. This is but the leaft.
The next will be a fatal ftroak, a blow indeed,
A thoufand Heads to lofe is not fo dreadful,
Let *Rutland* fee him at the very Moment
Of her expiring Husband ; fhe will hang
Worfe than his Guilt upon him, lure his Mind,
And pull it back to Earth again ; double
All the fierce Pangs of Thought and Death upon him,
And make his loaded Spirits fink to Hell.
   Queen. O th'art the *Machiavel* of all the Sex,
Thou braveft, moft heroick for Invention !
Come, let's difpatch————

     Enter Burleigh, Rawleigh, *Lords, Attendants, and Guards.*

My Lords, fee Execution done on *Effex* ;
But for *Southampton,* I will pardon him ;
His Crimes he may repent of ; they were not
So great, but done in friendfhip to the other.
Act my Commands with fpeed, that both of us
May ftraight be out of Torment————My Lord *Burleigh,*
And you Sir *Walter Rawleigh* fee't perform'd ;
I'll not return till you have brought the News.
                    [Exeunt Queen *and* Nottingham.
   R w. I wou'd fhe were a hundred Leagues from hence,
Well, and the Crown upon her Head ; I fear
She'll not continue in this mind a Moment.
   Burl. Then't fhall be done this Moment————Who attends ?
Bid the Lieutenant have his Prifoners ready.   *[Exit Officer*
Now we may hope to fee fair days again
In *England,* when this hov'ring Cloud is vanifht,
Which hung fo long betwixt our Royal Sun
And us, but foon will vifit us with Smiles,
And raife her drooping Subjects Hearts————

     Enter the two Earls, the Lieutenant and Guards
My Lord,
We bring an Order for your Execution,
And hope you are prepar'd ; for you muft dye
This very hour.   *South*

South. Indeed the time is fudden !——

Eff. Is Death th' Event of all my flatter'd Hopes!
Falfe Sex, and Queen more perjur'd than them all!
But dye I will without the leaft Complaint,
My Soul fhall vanifh filent as the Dew
Attracted by the Sun from verdent Fields,
And Leaves of weeping Flowers——Come, my dear Friend
Partner in Fate, give me thy Body in
Thefe faithful Arms, and O now let me tell thee,
And you, My Lords, and Heav'n my Witnefs too,
I have no weight, no heavinefs on my Soul,
But that I've loft my deareft Friend his Life.

South. And I proteft by the fame Powers Divine,
And to the World, 'tis all my happinefs,
The greateft Blifs my Mind yet e're enjoy'd,
Since we muft dye, my Lord, to dye together.

Burl. The *Queen*, my Lord *Southampton*, has been pleas'd
To grant particular mercy to your Perfon;
And has by us fent you a Reprieve from Death,
With Pardon of your Treafons, and commands
You to depart immediately from hence.

South. O my unguarded Soul ! Sure never was
A man with mercy wounded fo before!

Eff. Then I am loofe to fteer my wandring Voyage,
Like a glad Veffel that has long been croft,
And bound by adverfe Winds, at laft gets liberty,
And joyfully makes all the Sail fhe can,
To reach its wifh'd for Part—— Angels protect
The *Queen*; for her my chiefeft Prayers fhall be,
That as in time fh'as fpar'd my noble Friend,
And owns his Crimes worth mercy, may fhe ne're
Think fo of me too late when I am dead ——
Again *Southampton*, let me hold thee faft,
For 'tis my laft Embrace.

South. O be lefs kind, my Friend, or move lefs Pity,
Or I fhall fink beneath the weight of Sadnefs;
Witnefs the Joy I have in Life to part
With you; witnefs thefe Womans Throbs and Tears;
I weep that I am doom'd to live without you,
And fhou'd have fmil'd to fhare the Death of *Effex*.

Eff. O fpair this tendernefs for one that needs it,
For her that I'll commit to all that I
Can claim of my *Southampton*——O my Wife !
Methinks that very name fhou'd ftop thy Pity,
And make thee Covetous of all as loft
That is not meant to her ——Be a kind Friend
To her, as we have been to one another;

Name not the dying *Eſſex* to thy Queen
Leaſt it ſhou'd coſt a Tear, nor ne're offend her.
    South. O ſtay, my Lord, let me have one word more,
One laſt farewel before the greedy Axe
Shall part my Friend, my only Friend from me,
And *Eſſex* from himſelf———I know not what
Are call'd the Pangs of Death, but ſure I am
I feel an Agony that's worſe than Death———
Farewell.
    Eſſ. Why that's well ſaid——Farewell to thee———
Then let us part, juſt like two Travellers
Take diſtant Paths, only this difference is,
Thine is the longeſt, mine the ſhorteſt way.———
Now let me go———If there's a Throne in Heaven
For the moſt brave of Men and beſt of Friends,
I will beſpeak it for *Southampton*.
    South. And I, while I have life will Hoard thy Memory;
When I am dead, we then ſhall meet again.
    Eſſ. Till then Farewell.
    South. Till then Farewell.
    Eſſ. Now on my Lords, and execute your Office——— [*E*

Enter Counteſs of Eſſex *and Women.*

My Wife! Nay then my **Stars** will ne're have done.
Malicious Planets reign, I'll bear it all
To your laſt drop of Venom on my Head———
Why cruel Lovely Creature doſt thou come
To add to Sorrow if't be Poſſible :
A Figure more lamenting ? *Why this kindneſs,*
This killing kindneſs now at ſuch a time ?
To add more Woes to thine and my misfortunes.
    C. Eſſ. The Queen my Lord has been ſo merciful,
Or cruel, name it as you pleaſe, to let
Me ſee my *Eſſex* e're he dies.
    Eſſ. Has ſhe ?
Then let's improve this very little time
Our niggard Fate allows us : For w'are owing
To this ſhort ſpace all the dear love we had
In ſtore for many happy promis'd years.
    C. Eſſ. What hinders then but that we ſhou'd be happy,
Whilſt others live long years, and ſip, and taſte,
Like Niggards of their Loves, we'll take whole Draughts.
    Eſſ. Then let's embrace in Extaſies and Joys,
Drink all our Honey up in one ſhort moment,
That ſhou'd have ſerv'd us for our Winter-ſtore,
Be laviſh and profuſe like wanton Heirs

That wafte their whole Eftates at once,
For the kind Queen takes Care and has ordain'd
That we fhall never live to want.
  Burl. My Lord,
Prepare, the very utmoft time's at hand,
And we muft ftraight perform the Queens Command
In leading you to Juftice.
  C. *Eff.* Hold, good *Lucifer !*
Be kind a little, and defer Damnation,
Thou canft not think how I will worfhip thee,
No *Indian* fhall adore thee as I will,
Thou fhalt have Martyrs, and whole Hecatomb's
Of flaughter'd Innocents to fuck their Blood,
Widows Eftates and Orphans without number,
Mannors and Parks more than thy Luft requires,
Till thou fhalt dye and leave a King's Eftate
Behind thee.
  Eff. Pr'y thee fpare thy precious Heart,
That fluttering fo with Paffion in thy Breaft,
Has almoft bruis'd its tendernefs to Death.
  C. *Eff.* Why ask I him, and think of Pity there !
From him on whom kind Heav'n has fet a Mark,
A heap of Rubbifh at the Door to fhew
No cleanly Virtue can inhabit there————
Malicious Toad, and which is worfe, foul *Cecil,*
I tell thee *Effex* foon fhall reign in Heav'n,
While thou fhalt grovel in the Den of Hell ;
Roar like the Damn'd, and tremble to behold him.
Go fhare Dominions with the Powers of Hell ;
For *Lucifer* himfelf will ne're difpute
Thy great Defert in wickednefs above him,
Nor who's the uglier Fiend, thy felf or he.
  Raw. My Lord, you think not of the Queens Commands,
And can you ftand thus unconcern'd, and hear
Your felf fo much abus'd ?
  Burl. Be patient, *Rawleigh,*
The pain is all her own, and hurts not *Cecil,*
She will be weary fooner than my felf————
Poor innocent and moft unhappy Lady,
I pity her.
  C. *Eff.* Why, doft thou pity me !
Nay then I'm faln into a low Eftate
Indeed ; if Hell compaffionates my Miferies,
They muft be greater than the damn'd indure————}
I prithee pardon me————Ah my lov'd Lord,
My heart begins to break ; let me go with thee,
And fee the fatal blow given to my *Effex,*

That will be sure to rid me soon of Torments ;
And 'twill be kindness in thee———do, my Lord,
Then we shall both be quit of pain together.

Eff. Ah, why was I condemn'd to this, what Man
But *Essex* ever felt a weight like this !

C. Eff. O we must never part———Support my Head,
My sinking Head, and lay it to the Pulse,
The throbbing Pulse that beats about thy Heart,
'Tis Musick to my Sences———O my Love !
I have no tears left in me that shou'd ease
A wretch that longs for Pity———I am past
All Pity, and my poor tormented Heart,
And Spirits within are quite consum'd : and Tears
Which is the Balm, the Scorpions Blood that cures
The biting pain of Sorrow, quite have left me,
And I am now a wretched hopeless Creature,
Full of substantial Misery, without
One drop of Remedy.

Eff. Th'art pale, thy Breath
Grows chill, and like the Morning Air on Roses,
Leaves a cold Dew upon thy redder Lips.———
She strives, and holds me like a drowning wretch———
O now, my Lords, if pity ever blest you,
If you were never nurst by Tigers, help me———
Now, now, you cruel Heav'ns ! I plainly see,
'Tis not your Swords, your Axes, nor Diseases,
Which make the Death of Man so fear'd, and painful,
But 'tis such horrid Accidents as these———
She opens her Eyes, which with a waining look,
Like sickly Stars give a faint glimmering Light.

C. Eff. Where is my Love !
O think not to get loose, for I'm resolv'd,
To stick more close to thee than Life; and when
That's going, mine shall run the Race with thine,
And both together reach the happy Goal.

Eff. Now I am shock'd, torn up, and rooted all
That's Humane in me———What, you merciless Heavens
What is't that makes poor Man distracted, mad,
Prophane, to curse the Day, himself, the Heavens
That made him, but less miseries than mine ?
Why, why you Powers do you exact from Man
More than your World and all that live beside :
The Sea is never calm when Tempests blow,
Tall Woods and Cedars murmur at the Wind,
And when your horrid Earth-quakes cleave the Ground,
The Center groans, and Nature takes its part,
As if they did design to break your Laws,

And shake your Fetters off; nay your own Heavens
When Thunders roar, Rebel, the Sun ingages,
And all the warring Elements refift:
Heav'n, Seas, and Land are fuffer'd to contend,
But man alone is curft if he complain——
Farewell my everlafting Love, 'tis vain,
'Tis all in vain againft refiftlefs Fate
That pulls me from thee.   [*Gives her a Letter.*
Here, give this Paper to the Queen, which when
She reads, perhaps fhe will be kind to thee.
   C. *Eff.* Wilt thou not let me go?
I am prepar'd to fee the deadly ftroak,
And at that time the Fatal Axe falls on thee,
It will be fure to cut the twifted Cord
Of both our Lives afunder,
   Eff. We muft part——
Thou Miracle of Love, and Virtues all,
Farewell, and may thy *Effex* fad Misfortunes
Be doubl'd all in Bleffings on thy Soul——
Still, ftill thou grafps me like th' Pangs of Death——
Ha! now fhe faints, and like a Wretch
Striving to climb a fteep, and flippery Breach,
With many hard Attemtps gets up, and ftill
Slides down again, fo fhe lets go at laft
Her eager hold, and finks beneath her weight——
Support her all——
   Burl. My Lord fhe will recover;
Pray leave her with her Woman, and make ufe
Of this fo kind an Opportunity
To part with her.
   Eff. Cruel hard-hearted *Burleigh*!
Moft Barbarous *Cecil.*
   Burl. See, my Lord,
She foon will come t'her felf, and you muft leave her——
Hafte away.
   Lieut. Make way there.
   Eff. Look to her, faithful Servants, while fhe lives
She'll be a tender Miftrefs to you all——
Come, pufh me off then, fince I muft Swim o're,
Why do I ftand thus fhivering on the Shore!
'Tis but a Breath, and I no more fhall think,
Mix with the Sun or into Attoms fhrink:
Lift up thy Eyes no more in fearch of mine,
Till I am dead, then glad the World with thine——
This kifs (O that it wou'd for ever laft!)
Gives me of Immortality a Taft——
Farewel,

May all that's paft when thou recover'ft feem
Like a glad waking from a fearful Dream.

*Exeunt*Eſſex *to Execution,* Burleigh, Rawleigh, *Lieut. and Guards.*
[*Manent Counteſs of* Eſſex *with Women.*

Wom. See, ſhe revives.
C. *Eſſ.* Where is my *Eſſex,* where?
Wom. Alas! I fear by this time he's no more.
C. *Eſſ.* Why did you wake me then from ſuch bright Objects?
I ſaw my *Eſſex* mount with Angels wings
(Whilſt I rode on the beauteous Cherubin,)
And took me on 'em, bore me o're the World
Through everlaſting Skies, Eternal Light.
Wom. Be Comforted.
C. *Eſſ.* Sure we're the only Pair
Can boaſt of ſuch a Pomp of Miſery,
And none was e're ſubſtantially ſo curſt,
Since the firſt Couple that knew Sorrow firſt;
Yet they were happy, and for Paradice
Found a new World unskill'd, unfraught with Vice,
No Tyrant to moleſt 'em, nor no Sword,
All that had Life Obedience did afford,
No Pride but Labour there and healthful Pains,
No Thief to rob them of their honeſt Gains:
Ambition now the Plague of ev'ry Thought,
Then was not known, or elſe was unbegot.

Enter the Queen, Counteſs of Nottingham, *Lords and Attendants.*

Queen. Behold where the poor *Rutland* lyes, almoſt
As dead, and low as *Eſſex* in his Grave
Can be, and I want but a very little
To be more miſerable than 'em both———
Rife, rife unfortunate and mournful *Rutland,*
I know not what to call thee now, but wiſh
I could not call thee by the name of *Eſſex*———
Rife, and behold thy Queen, I ſay,
That bends to take thee in her Arms.
C. *Eſſ.* O never think to charm me with ſuch ſounds,
Such hopes that are too diſtant from my Soul,
For 'tis but Preaching Heav'n to one that's Damn'd———
O take your Pity back, moſt cruel Queen,
Give it to thoſe that want it for a Cure,
My griefs are Mortal, Remedies are vain,
And thrown away on ſuch a wretch as I———
Here is a Paper from my Lord to you,
It was his laſt Requeſt that you would Read it.

Queen

Queen. Giv't me——but oh how much more welcom had
The Ring been in its ſtead.　　　　　　　　　*[Reads to her ſelf.]*
　　C. Nott. Ha! I'm betray'd.　　　　　　　　　　*[Aſide.]*
　　Queen. Haſte, ſee if Execution yet be done,
If not, prevent it——Fly with Angels Wings——　　*[Officer goes*
Oh thou far worſe than Serpent——worſe than Woman!　*out.*
Ah *Rutland!* here's the Cruel cauſe of both our Woes,
Mark this, and help to Curſe her for thy Husband.

　　　　　　　The Queen reads the Letter.

Madam,

I Receive my Death with the Willingneſs and Submiſſion of a Subject, and
　　as it is the will of Heav'n and of Your Majeſty, with this Requeſt that
you wou'd be pleas'd to beſtow that Royal Pity on my Poor Wife which is deny'd to me, and my laſt flying Breath ſhall bleſs you. I have but one Thing
to repent of ſince my Sentence, which is, that I ſent the Ring by Nottingham, fearing it ſhou'd once put my Queen in mind of her broken Vow.
　　　　　　　　　　　　　　　　　　　　　　　　　Eſſex.

Repentance, Horrors, Plagues, and deadly Poyſons,
Worſe than a thouſand Deaths torment thy Soul.
　　C. Nott. Madam———
　　Queen. Condemn me firſt to hear the Groans of Ghoſts,
The Croaks of Ravens, and the damn'd in Torments,
Juſt Heav'n, 'tis Muſick to what thou can'ſt utter;
Begone———Fly to that utmoſt verge of Earth,
Where the Globe's bounded with Eternity,
And never more be ſeen of humane kind,
Curſt with long Life, and with a fear to dye,
With thy Guilt ever in thy Memory,
And *Eſſex* Ghoſt be ſtill before thy Eye.
　　C. Nott. I do confeſs———
　　Queen. Quick, bear her from my ſight, her words are blaſting,
Her Eyes are Baſilisks, infection reigns
Where e're ſhe breaths; go ſhut her in a Cave,
Or chain her to ſome Rock whole Worlds from hence,
The diſtance is too near; there let her live
Howling to th' Seas to rid her of her pain,
For ſhe and I muſt never meet again———
Away with her.
　　C. Nott. I go——but have this comfort in my Doom;
I leave you all with greater Plagues at home.　　　　*[Exit Nott.*

　　　　　　　Enter Burleigh *and* Rawleigh.

Burl. Madam your Orders came too late———
The Earl was Dead———
　　Queen. Then I wiſh thou wer't dead that ſay'ſt it;

　　　　　　　　　　　　　　　　　　　　　　　　　But

But I'll be juft, and curfe none but my felf———
What faid he when he came fo foon to dye?

Burl. Indeed his End, made fo by woful Cafualties,
Was very fad and full of Pity,
But at the block all Hero he appear'd,
Or elfe to give him a more Chriftian Title,
A Martyr arm'd with Refolution,
Said little, but did blefs your Majefty,
And dy'd full of Forgivenefs to the World,
As was no doubt his Soul that foon expir'd.

Queen. Come thou choice Relict of lamented *Effex,*
Call me no more by th' name of Queen, but Friend.
When thy dear Husband's Death Reveng'd fhall be,
Pity my Fate, but lay no Guilt on me,
Since 'tis th' Almighty's Pleafure, though fevere,
To punifh thus his Faithful Regents here,
To lay on Kings his hardeft Task of Rule,
And yet has given 'em but a Humane Soul.
The fubtil Paths of Traytors Hearts to view,
Reafon's too dark, a hundred Eyes too few;
Yet when by Subjects we have been betray'd,
The blame is ours, their Crimes on us are laid,
And that which makes a Monarch's happinefs,
Is not in Reigning well, but with Succefs.

[*Exeunt Omnes*

EPI-

EPILOGUE,

By Mr. *DRYDEN.*

WE *Act by Fits and Starts, like drowning Men,*
     But juſt peep up, and then drop down again ;
Let thoſe who call us Wicked change their ſence,
For never men liv'd more on Providence,
Nor Lott'ry Cavilers are half ſo poor,
Nor Broken Cits, nor a Vacation Whore,
Not Courts nor Courtiers living on the Rents
Of the three laſt ungiving Parliaments.
So wretched, that if Pharaoh *could Divine*
He might have ſpar'd his Dream of ſeven lean Kine,
And chang'd the Viſion for the Muſes Nine.
The Comet which they ſay portends a Dearth,
Was but a Vapour drawn from Play-houſe Earth,
Pent here ſince our laſt Fire, and Lilly *ſays,*
Foreſhows our change of State and thin third days.
'Tis not our want of Wit that keeps us poor,
For then the Printers Preſs would ſuffer more :
Their Pamphletcers their Venom daily ſpit,
They thrive by Treaſon, and we ſtarve by Wit.
Confeſs the truth, which of you has not laid
Four Farthings out to buy the Hatfield *Maid ?*
Or what is duller yet, and more does ſpite us,
Democritus *his Wars with* Heraclitus *?*
Theſe are the Authors that have run us down,
And Exerciſe you Criticks of the Town ;
Yet theſe are Pearls to your Lampooning Rhimes,
Y' abuſe your ſelves more dully than the Times ;
Scandal, the Glory of the Engliſh *Nation,*
Is worn to Rags, and Scribled out of Faſhion ;
Such harmleſs Thruſts, as if like Fencers Wiſe,
You had agree'd your Play before the Prize.
Faith you may hang your Harps upon the Willows,
'Tis juſt like Children when they box with Pillows.
Then put an end to Civil Wars for ſhame,
Let each Knight Errant who has wrong'd a Dame,
Throw down his Pen, and give her if he can,
The ſatisfaction of a Gentleman.

To the up-
per Gallery.

PRO-

PROLOGUE,

Intended to be spoken, Written by the Author.

'TIS *said when the Renown'd* Augustus *Reign'd,*
  That all the World in Peace and Wealth remain'd,
And though the School of Action, War was o're,
Arms, Arts, and Letters then increas'd the more.
All these sprung from our Royal Virgins Bays,
And flourish'd better than in Cæsar's *Days ;*
And only in her time at once was seen
So brave a Souldier, States-man, and a Queen.   Essex and Burleigh.
Her Reign may be compar'd to that above,
As the best Poet, Cæsar's *did to* Jove :
For as great Julius *built the mighty'st Throne,*
And left Rome's *first large Empire to his Son,*
Under whose weight, till Her, we all did groan ;
So her great Father was the first that struck
Rome's *Triple Crown ; but she threw off the Yoak :*
Straight at her Birth new Light the Heav'ns adorn'd,
Which more than Fifteen hundred Years had mourn'd, ———
But hold, I'm bid to let you understand,
That when our Poet took this Work in Hand,
He trembl'd straight, like Prophets in a Dream,
Her awful Genius stood, and threaten'd him,
Her modest Beauties only he has shown,
And has her Character so nicely drawn,
That if her self in purest Robes of Light,
Shou'd come from Heav'n, and bless us with her sight,
She would not blush to hear what he has Writ.
Therefore ———
To all the shining Sex this Play's addrest,
But more the Court, *the Planets of the Rest ;*
You who on Earth are Man's best, sofest Fate,
So that when Heav'n with some ruff Peace has met,
It sends him you to mould, and new Create.
Strange ways to Virtue, some may think to prove,
But yet the best and surest Path is Love,
Love like the Ermine, is so nice a Guest,
It never enters in a vitious Breast ———
If you are pleas'd, we will be bold to say,
This modest Poem is the Ladies Play.

FINIS.

0 1341 1463878 3

CPSIA information can be obtained at www.ICGtesting.com
Printed in the USA
LVOW111721210613

339730LV00009B/325/P

9 781240 861521